A Journey in Faith

An Experience
of the Catechumenate

Raymond B. Kemp

Sadlier
A Division of William H. Sadlier, Inc.
New York
Chicago
Los Angeles

2

*To the People of Saints Paul and
Augustine Parish—their story*

Nihil Obstat
Reverend Lorenzo Albacete
Censor Deputatus
Imprimatur
✠ William Cardinal Baum
Archbishop of Washington
June 6, 1979
The nihil obstat and imprimatur are official declarations that a book or
pamphlet is free of doctrinal or moral error. No implication is contained
therein that those who have granted the nihil obstat and imprimatur agree
with the contents, opinions, or statements expressed.

Home Office:
11 Park Place
New York, N.Y. 10007
ISBN: 0-8215-9329-3
123456789/9

Contents

Personal Preface

I am the kind of person who enjoys hearing the professor begin a course with a recital of both expectations and biases. The need to place this book in the personal context of my hopes and dreams cannot be avoided. For what follows grows out of being a priest for ten years in the same parish. And it grows out of faith shared by some beautiful Catholics who have been part of that time and by those who were part of earlier years of formation during the time of Vatican Council II.

This experience comes from a contemporary falling-out not with the Church but with establishmentarianism during the *Humanae Vitae* controversy and a falling into social action and elected politics while remaining an assistant pastor at Saints Paul and Augustine Parish in Washington, D.C. It comes, as much, from falling more deeply in love with the Church during a leisurely vacation tour from Rome to Paris a few years ago. I saw the Church at work in the Vatican and in the coffeehouse run by a priest for working prostitutes in Paris. I saw it in the peace movement that sprang from sources like the Catholic Worker. But most of all this work springs from being one of a number of priests in a proud but struggling Black Catholic parish.

This book, in the long run, is not mine. It is the accumulation of intimate contact with persons of faith and their experiences. It grows as well from the successes and failures of the catechetical enterprise of many in our parish. Finally it is a reaction to the slow but steady stream of people looking for religion and for Jesus. It was this above all that formed a book in the head and the heart of the author, and it had to find a way to paper.

The mystery of ministry in the Catholic Church for me is that when a lay person or priest says, "I am available to you," there are folks who turn up seeking what you have to offer and give as much back as you are prepared to give them.

It was just a few years ago that I literally grabbed a copy of the first English translation of the *Rite of Christian Initiation of Adults* from one who had a copy of the early provisional text. At Saints Paul and Augustine we needed direction in our convert classes. Awareness of the document led to inquiry, study, and practical questions. How can the Rite of Christian Initiation make a difference in Catholic faith life? How can it be implemented? Above all, what does it mean?

For us at Saints Paul and Augustine the Rite has been a gold mine of inspiration. The past few years have seen the parish implement most of the elements of the Rite in the spirit if not the letter in which it appears.

I used to have a problem with rites and rituals, probably an effect of fairly strict instruction in celebrating the rite of Mass. But the *Rite of Christian Initiation of Adults* is more than a manual for convert-making. It is, rather, a process of unfolding personality and coming to faith. It transcends the widely accepted notion of rite. The key word is "process." Using the process built into the Rite has helped me appreciate the spiritual growth moments that are the life of the Church in sacraments. The rites of religion, the rites of spring, the rituals of love, of politics, of personal posturing—all are elemental to life and incredibly important to one who values symbols and sacraments as the edge of real life.

At first the language and the vocabulary of this Rite put me off. I felt as strange with *precatechumenate, enlightenment, election, purification,* and *mystagogia* as some of my older colleagues had felt, I am sure, with *president of the assembly, sense of community,* and *reconciliation.* Yet those words take flesh, too, and the mystery of the words soon become the mystery of the experience.

The book, *A Journey in Faith,* is simple and direct. It has sparse footnotes and limited bibliography. A copy of the *Rite of Christian Initiation of Adults*[1] should be at hand as you read because I feel no need to reprint it here. A Bible may help later. But your experiences of being involved in the ministry of religious education, coming to an adult sense of faith, or being a convert yourself is all you need to master this book. *A Journey in Faith* is not in the genre of "how to start a catechumenate in your parish in a few easy lessons." Rather, this book is how and why we at Saints Paul and Augustine are doing what we are doing for those who seek a deepening of faith. It is also a bit about what we know needs doing that we have not done.

It is the combined experience of early convert classes and later experiences of catechumenate that created this book. So it is to those good women and men with whom I have had the privilege of journeying that it is dedicated and to the hope that our parish will continue as we have begun in faith and love. If our experience can be shared by others in their ministry of conversion and renewal, then *A Journey in Faith* shall have achieved its goal.

Raymond B. Kemp, Pastor
Saints Paul and Augustine

[1] Provisional Text (Study Book Edition), 1974, USCC, 1312 Massachusetts Ave., N.W., Washington, D.C., 20005.

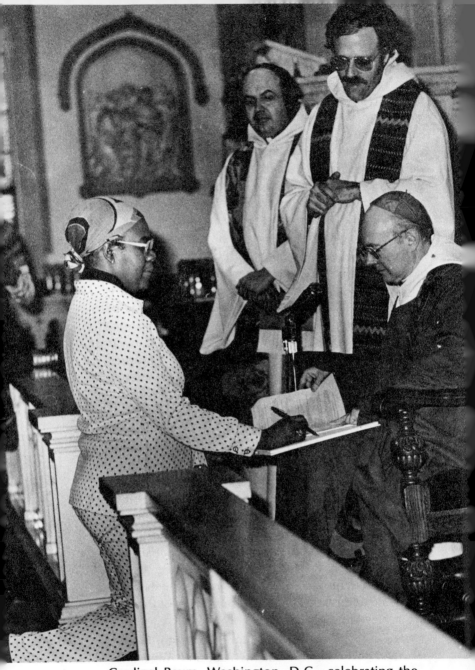

Cardinal Baum, Washington, D.C., celebrating the rite of Election in the parish of Saints Paul and Augustine.

Overview

Inquiry and Convert Class Background

Instructions in the Catholic Faith

A new class is forming for those interested in becoming Catholic or in reviewing the basics of their Catholic faith. The first meeting will be on next Thursday night at 7:30 P.M. in the Rectory. The class will meet weekly for twenty weeks. All are invited.

Such an announcement used to be a semiannual item in most parish bulletins. If your parish did not run a class, the priest made himself available for the instruction of individuals. In cities that had such, he referred interested non-Catholics to the Catholic Information Center for a sixteen-, twenty-, or twenty-four-week course that could lead to reception into the Church or Baptism.

As an introduction to priestly ministry, many a newly ordained received, along with the teen club and the altar boys, the "convert class" assignment.

The priest normally picked the textbook for the convert class, usually of question-and-answer format, or considered himself progressive and industrious by making and dittoing his own notes. Whether the course was termed inquiry, convert, or basic beliefs, it was a series of sessions with the priest as teacher and final arbiter of any controversy. In the words of one outworn classic in the field, the approach was "Father Smith Instructs Jackson." Whether oriented to an individual or to a group of five or twenty-five, the teacher-student model was normative, with time for discussion.

There was a catechism, or some such book to be "covered," and prayers to be memorized. Mastery of those doctrinal formulations specifically Catholic was what was really urged. In a fairly neat package the elemental content of the deposit of faith was put in the minds of the listeners. And it worked—for many.

"Converts make the best Catholics," it was often said. "She has been a Catholic for only three years, and she is head of the Altar Society."

The duration of the course was left to the judgment of the priest or the custom of the parish. Diocesan authorities or agencies rarely made any attempt to regularize either length or content of the course. If twenty weeks were promised, twenty weeks they got, whether or not the class got snagged for three weeks on the hypostatic union. Father or another priest would always be available after class to answer your questions.

The reception or Baptism of the new Catholic was usually performed privately by the priest with the family of the newly baptized. Until just a few years ago, the newly received adult was scheduled for Confirmation whenever the bishop made his rounds of the parishes. The adult convert came at the end of the Confirmation line after the sixth graders with the same sponsors as the CCD or Catholic school children. Or the convert was sent to the cathedral on Pentecost, when the bishop confirmed adults who somehow had escaped Confirmation in their earlier years. And the converts returned to the priest and to anyone else they knew to report that they were now "full" Catholics, as complete as any who had been born and raised such!

The follow-up program was largely determined by the priest. The "program" ranged from casual questions after Mass ("How is it going?") to advanced courses in liturgy, Scripture, dogma, or morality. The priest who ran the introductory course leading to Baptism stressed that he was full-time in the parish in order to deal with their questions or problems. If experience is any indicator, he usually heard from at least a portion of his new converts during the first years.

The best follow-up programs were in those parishes that had the gift of recruiting new converts to some parish organization. In our parish, the Sodality ladies enrolled the newly baptized women and, as a matter of course, registered them for a further year of candidate classes to make them full-fledged Sodalists.

Convert classes in most parishes ran twice a year, or in large parishes two classes ran simultaneously for the convenience of working people. Although no sure statistics are available on the racial or economic makeup of the new converts, one could make an educated guess that in regions where Black Catholics were established, Black converts to Catholicity comprised the lion's share of adult baptisms in a given diocese as reported to the P.J. Kenedy *Catholic Directory* annually. It has been that way in Washington, D.C., since the 40s.

In the 60s from a few Black parishes and some native American Indian parishes we began to hear the word "catechumenate." When adult Baptism in seven stages was reintroduced for mission lands, a few urban parishes in the States began to use that ritual with their own adaptations. Yet relatively few articles or seminars appeared on the subject. Probably the few pioneers were too busy to make their voices heard. In suburban parishes, where the number of converts was small enough to be seated comfortably in a rectory office, there was seemingly little need to investigate the catechumenate-type programs, which seemed to have been reestablished with a foreign intent: to stamp out pagan religion and allegiance to tribal deities. That alien sense of weaning pygmies or warriors away from idols was what undoubtedly necessitated seven stages of initiation into the Catholic Church that spanned a year or more. Unfortunately that same sense of dealing with mission lands has prevented many pastorally involved persons from appreciating the newly restored rite.

In the last few years the chief emphasis in adult religious education in the United States has been geared to those who are already Catholic. Parish, diocesan, national, and publishing efforts have been directed to parental preparation for their children's reception of the sacraments, courses in appreciating the considerable impact of the Second Vatican Council on the life of the Church, and Scripture study. Moreover, elaborate and well designed programs were signs that we had come of age in liturgical ministry in many dioceses in the country. How many meetings did you attend on preparing Catholics for the new Rite of Reconciliation?

Efforts in areas related to instruction of converts have consisted of a few better catechisms and summaries of Catholic belief and a few revisions of older works that guarantee they are "in accord with the renewal of the Catholic Church as directed by the Second Vatican Council." But a favorite question among priests who meet in religious bookstores still is: "What are you using for converts?" And the truth of it seems to be that there is no one book to be used for converts whether you are referring to the semiliterate or to those with graduate degrees. Could it be that in a Church that claims to be apostolic, there is no market for an abundance of such materials?

The Rite of Christian Initiation: When?

On the feast of the Epiphany, January 6, 1972, Arture Cardinal Tabera, Prefect, and A. Bugnini, Secretary, of the Sacred Congregation for Divine Worship, affixed their signatures to a decree that introduced "a new rite for the Christian initiation of adults, which has been approved by Pope Paul VI." This rite was a direct result of the Council that had ended six and a half years earlier,[2] and we were ordered to use the rite in Latin immediately and in the vernacular upon completion of an approved translation.

From the time the rite was published in Latin until 1974 (two and a half years later), you had to have a friend on the International Committee on English in the Liturgy (ICEL) in order to obtain even a poorly xeroxed copy of the text. Then in 1974 the United States Catholic Conference published the *Rite of Christian Initiation of Adults,* a Provisional Text in a Study Book Edition. Copies are available from the Publications Office, United States Catholic Conference, 1312 Massachusetts Avenue, N.W., Washington, D.C. 20005. No commercial religious publisher has yet made the text of the Rite available in English with a commentary.

This present work is not a commentary on the text of the Rite but rather a pastoral reflection on how one parish has used the Rite. It is not the final word on how to implement the Rite from precatechumenate to mystagogia. *A Journey in Faith* presents the fruits of four years of gradual implementation of various elements of a delightfully flexible ritual in a parish in Washington, D.C. Its purpose is to further discussion among pastoral leadership on the variety of ways by which the *Rite of Christian Initiation of Adults* may be integrated into the life of a parish and to open our own local experience to the scrutiny and constructive criticism of the whole Church in the United States and elsewhere. In another five years we may be writing a totally different kind of book.

[2] *Constitution on the Sacred Liturgy,* 64.

The Restoration of the Rite of Christian Initiation: What?

LIKE every other sacramental revision from Vatican II, the meat and potatoes of this Christian initiation process is in its Introduction. It is fifteen pages long including the footnotes. It required four reflective readings on my part before I screamed "Eureka!" In our fifth year of doing it, little lights continue to go on in my brain from time to time, and words like "scrutinies" and "mystagogia" become realities with meaning. If you have not yet read the Introduction twice, read it now, or the rest of this treatment will throw you for a loss.

The reason we knew that the Rite was for us, the compelling part of those words on the page, is best summarized in the very last paragraph of the Introduction:

> It is for the celebrant to use fully and intelligently the freedom which is given to him either in the General Introduction (no. 34) or in the rubrics of the rite. In many places the manner of acting or praying is intentionally left undetermined or two possibilities are offered, so that the celebrant may accommodate the rite, according to his prudent pastoral judgment, to the circumstances of the candidates and others who are present. The greatest freedom is left in the introductions and intercessions, which may always be shortened, changed, or even increased with new intentions in order to correspond with

the circumstances or special situation of the candidates (for example, a sad or joyful event occurring in a family) or of the others present (for example, joy or sorrow common to the parish or town) (*RCIA*, 67).

That paragraph, headed "Adaptations by the Minister," follows closely an eight-part section on "Adaptations by Episcopal Conferences Which Use the Roman Ritual." Because I had been involved in convert work (along with altar boys and teen club), because I was stationed where I was and people kept coming to join the Church, because the five-month course of classes seemed somehow so incomplete, I came to feel—really *feel*—that the shapers of this ritual of Christian initiation were speaking to me and others like me. I could not remember the last time that I was asked to use my freedom fully and intelligently. Right now, within the general directives of the Rite, it is safe to assume that the freedom to introduce the whole Rite or parts thereof in the fashion most intelligible and intelligent to the candidate and the parish is wide open. Anything that is said here in no way limits that intelligent and prudent use of freedom.

With the last paragraph of the Rite as incentive to study the whole text, let us analyze what is described and distinguish some elements which could initially create confusion. The four stages of the Rite are the precatechumenate, the catechumenate, the period of purification and enlightenment which begins with "the election," and finally the period of postbaptismal catechesis or mystagogia. The rest of this book will explain these stages in greater detail. For now, a brief overview will suffice.

Four Stages

THE *precatechumenate,* the first stage of the Rite, is also called the period of evangelization, a topic that has been discussed by the Pope, the Synod of Bishops, our own Conference of Bishops, and individual theologians and catechists. It is a time of coming to know the Lord from those who proclaim Him. Just as evangelization is a constitutive part of the Church's mission in the world, so the openness of the parish to receiving those who have heard the Word and begun an initial conversion of life is given substance in the precatechumenate. It is a time for meeting, a time for hospitality. It is a time of getting to know the Lord and, in light of His Gospel, meeting oneself and beginning the "turn" toward Him. It is also a time when the candidate meets the families and the communities of Catholics which make up the local parish.

Precatechumenate, then, is the direct result of evangelization, presumably on the part of the local parish. Precatechumenate begins when the parish or Catholics in the parish believe that what they have received as a gift must be given as one, when the feeling is aroused in the non-believer or the non-Catholic that this Church is the community of faith where I may find the Lord. Precatechumenate is a time for meeting those who know the Lord and who in the community of the parish are doing the works of the Lord: prayer, worship, Christian service, works for justice, works of mercy, religious education. It is a time when the parish introduces itself and its Lord to the interested party and when the interested party—the candidate—assesses his or her life. The period ends with a decision to enter into the catechumenate proper.

The *catechumenate*, second stage of the process, is the time when the candidate becomes a Christian and is more fully introduced to the Christian faith and community through catechesis, celebration, prayer, and conversation. The goal of the catechumenate is the complete catechesis of the Gospel message. If the kerygma or first proclamation of the saving news is the purpose of the precatechumenate, then the goal of the catechumenate is nothing less than the fullest possible introducing of Jesus, His work and message, and how He fulfilled the Covenant, which He made His own. It is the time to understand the Scriptures and the Church of the Acts of the Apostles which authored the New Testament after preaching the Good News and bringing countless unbelievers to faith. Catechumenate is part of the journey in faith that every Christian and Catholic must make, from faith to a deeper understanding of life, of morality, of prayer and worship.

The catechumenate is what the Fathers of the Church preached on Sundays, not for ten minutes but for hours, in their churches. The catechumenate is what those artists in stained glass created in pictures in the great European cathedrals and churches. These visuals were meant to explain to those who could not read how God is saving us in Jesus and how we participate with the Christ in redeeming Yahweh's creation and giving the earth a sense of its purposefulness.

The catechumenate is the time when faith in the risen Lord and the scandal of the Cross are translated into the personal conviction that I mean something to God and that I can make a difference in the way of the world. It is journey, discovery, wonder, mystery, sorrow, joy. It is not an elaborate outline of history and creeds looking for someone to believe, but rather faith seeking understanding.

The catechumenate concludes when the catechesis is over. Time is no limit; it is a value. And it takes time to complete the catechesis to the point where the catechumens and the parish are excited and confident enough to decide mutually to initiate completely these candidates into the saving sacramental experience which is the Church. The decision on the part of the parish is called the "Election," the choice to baptize, confirm, and eucharist these candidates now to be called "elect." It is a solemn time, a true climax in the initial journey.

The election begins the *period of purification and enlightenment,* the next stage of the initiation process. The election no doubt springs from a genuine decision on the part of early Christian communities to join to themselves those catechumens who had shown the sincerity of their faith by participating fully in the catechumenal journey. *Those early parishioners knew their candidates through meeting them and participating in their formation directly, and they knew them from worship, sharing, singing, and praying with them during the Liturgy of the Word on Sundays.*

The formation of catechumens was, like the Eucharist itself, integral to those early churches. And, no doubt, as Lent approached, some candidates were elected to be initiated. Others, while encouraged to continue as members of the parish in catechumenate, were politely told they needed more time. It is interesting to note that the current revision provides for the Catholic marriage of catechumens, a clear indication that, as catechumen, he/she is a Christian and that the time question should present no problem if another year or more passes before one is initiated fully into the sacramental life of the Church.

The election symbolizes, too, the Christian's election to faith. It is something we cannot fathom, but we who believe are a chosen race. God's choice of Israel, His choice of those who believe in His Son, is mirrored in the choice of the community of faith and ratified and celebrated on the first Sunday of Lent ideally not by the pastor or the associate pastor involved with the catechumenate but by the ordinary or his delegate.

The Rite brings election to the fore of the bishop's ministry and clearly replaces his Confirmation role in the Easter Vigil Mass which is celebrated by the local parish with the local pastor.

The period of purification or enlightenment, an intensive phase of the initiation process, can best be understood by studying the purpose of Lent. The daily Lenten Masses, the texts for which were picked with "the elect" in mind, taken together with a A cycle of readings which include the scrutinies and the presentation of the Creed and the Lord's Prayer, set the program for this intensive phase. Self-assessment, examination of intentions, the spirit of repentance, and a heightened anticipation of the glorious victory celebration of Easter are essential to enlightenment and purification.

As a matter of fact, not of surmise or wondering, it is clear to me that Lent celebrated without the elect is but a shadow of what Lent ought to be. It is the season for those preparing to be initiated into the saving Body of Christ. Those already initiated are invited to reflect on their first enthusiasm for the faith in the presence of those to be baptized. Catholics are urged to self-examination and repentance, to fasting and works of justice and charity not only for their own good alone but also in support of and as example to the elect. The term "scrutinies" applies to the completion of the spiritual and catechetical preparation of the elect as they prepare for the feast of Easter and for the sacraments of initiation. Their purpose is mainly spiritual and they are intended "to purify the catechumens' minds and hearts, to strengthen them against temptation, and to purify their intentions, and to make firm their decision, so that they remain more closely united with Christ and make progress in their efforts to love God more deeply. These rites, mostly exorcisms, are celebrated on the third, fourth, and fifth Sundays of Lent" (RCIA, 153, 154).

The most basic motivation for the Catholics' active participation in Lenten liturgies and programs is to be a concrete and living sign to the elect of how this local parish can embody what Christian life is about: prayer, fasting, self-denial for the work of redeeming the face of the earth. We can do those things for our own salvation, but how much more meaningful they become when, instead of merely serving self, we are serving those whom we are preparing for full membership and initiation into our community!

The whole emphasis is thus changed for the Catholic, and the renewal of baptismal promises at the Easter Vigil is done out of a spirit of having traveled that journey in faith again with those who are making the trip for the first time. Lent, as a time for the reinitiation of the Catholic, becomes clear in the presence of the elect.

The period of election is brought to a close with the Solemn Easter Vigil, and the holiness of that night is heightened by a meeting earlier in the day with the elect, their sponsors, their relatives, friends and other interested parishioners. It is a time of prayer, of practice, and of joy muted only by the Good Friday-Holy Saturday fast. The parish party which follows the Vigil, a true *break fast,* is the time for the informal festive gathering.

The period of postbaptismal catechesis or mystagogia, the final stage of the initiation, demands a renewed appreciation of the Church's Easter celebration. The fifty days between Easter and Pentecost are as important to the life of the parish as the forty days of Lent. Lent and Easter time are the "before and after," the fast and the celebration of the whole Church year. And how few parishes have begun to place them in tandem to experience what one does for the other and what the newly baptized do for the celebration of Lent and Easter time!

In the best of all possible worlds, the conclusion of the catechumenate ends anything approaching classwork. Lent and the Easter season, for the elect who become neophytes, and for the parish itself, is a communal reflection and sharing of the meaning of the sacraments, of scriptural witness as well as personal witness to the power of Christ and His Gospel to change the course of history—my history merges into your history, and becomes *our* history—the history of our salvation.

These sessions of celebration of the Eucharist are times of shared prayer and Scripture readings, leading to works of mercy and action for justice. They are as well times of discussion and the stretching of imagination and faith vistas and are among the most precious in the life of the local church, more fascinating than anyone's design for a Lenten Program or a Spring Course in Catholicism. The time of postbaptismal sharing is called "mystagogia." It is an ongoing, life-oriented catechesis.

This is the Church renewing itself annually in the blood of the Lamb and in the context of its evangelical and apostolic calling. And whether the whole parish is involved or just a very few, it is a sign and foretaste of what our parishes can become.

The postbaptismal catechesis is a shared explanation and teaching by catechists, parishioners, and beginners together of the power of the risen Christ fully to save and reorient every nook and cranny of our lives. It is teaching, but the kind of teaching that comes from experience; and everyone is student and teacher for everyone else. This is what they mean when they say "You are the Church." More than any parish council meeting or priests senate conference, more than any congress of charismatics or cursillistas, more than any Eucharistic Congress or national family life convention, these Sunday liturgies of Easter and the sessions for postbaptismal catechesis are to be the Church fully alive!

And this is an area that we have yet to develop because we are just beginning to see the tip of what is in store for us.

Practical Considerations

THE revised Rite of Christian Initiation clearly is seen as the operation of the local parish in totality. How can parishes of a thousand families or ten thousand worshipers ever attempt to make a catechumenate its own?

The catechumenate is restored to be "adapted to contemporary missionary work throughout the world" (RCIA, 2). While it is obviously designed for the unbapitzed, its fourth chapter makes provisions for preparing baptized but uncatechized adults for Confirmation and the Eucharist in much the same way as the catechumenate approach, but "their conversion is based on the baptism they have already received, and they must unfold its power" (RCIA, 295). What do we do about those baptized in other Christian churches? When they approach the Catholic Church seeking membership, are they considered "insiders" or "outsiders"? And what of the many unbaptized who have experienced as much religious education as many Catholics in the message of Jesus? Are they to be treated in the same manner as those who have just heard of Jesus? Can a catechist mix the unbaptized, the baptized non-Catholic, and the Catholic seeking a personal renewal together?

Finally, how do you begin the conversion from inquiry class to catechumenate in terms of recruitment and timing of the stages? Can one parish begin a year-long catechumenate when the next parish clings to a four- or five-month course? How do you recruit for so ambitious a catechumenate as a year or more, especially if the number of "converts" in your parish is small or almost nil?

Let us tackle these preliminary questions and considerations briefly enough to allay some fears and keep you reading. These are questions that more authoritative persons in the Church will eventually have to address as the necessity for minimal standards arises. Right now we are "on our own," and our experiences should prove most helpful to those who will be developing such guidelines. They will indeed need our experience in order to speak to real concerns of local parishes.

First, the whole parish is not likely to get completely involved in the formation of new members just as the whole parish is not involved in Sunday Eucharist. Small parishes may more readily attain the goal of the Rite to involve the whole community. But larger and smaller parishes can certainly find adult Catholics who want and need such an ecclesial experience as the catechumenate. These adult members who desire a renewal of Christian life may already have been exposed to other renewal efforts or movements in the life of the Church and may well be ready to "learn while doing" in a ministry to potential catechumens. These Catholics and those who are part of the leadership of the parish play a key role as representatives of the whole parish.

Next, the liturgies which involve catechumens, elect, or neophytes center-stage must be the result of planning for the whole parish. Ideally, by the time of the Easter Vigil Mass, the persons in the pews should at least a dozen times or so have seen, met, and prayed for those desiring entrance. The impact of these initiation liturgies on longtime Catholics and on converts from the days of the inquiry class cannot be underestimated. People in the pews do get involved, and representatives of the whole parish are fully involved in this formative process.

The question of how to treat the unbaptized and the baptized non-Catholic could get a little tricky, especially if you copy prayers out of a ritual onto a mimeograph stencil. This process is meant to be accommodated to your parish situation. For the Catholic and the baptized non-Catholic, the process unfolds what is already theirs. For the unbaptized, the process unfolds what has been there for two thousand years.

Should you rebaptize those already baptized in another Christian church? Never. The Rite is strict on that question alone. But may you anoint a baptized non-Catholic with the oil of catechumens? Why not, if the anointing expresses a special consecration and openness to catechesis. May you scrutinize the intentions of baptized and unbaptized at the same time? It appears from the rite of the scrutinies that the intentions of those already baptized as Catholics and preparing for Easter are as much a concern in the prayer of the Church as are those to be baptized.

If we seem to fudge a little on what is "on the inside looking out or the outside looking in," it is because once a person becomes a catechumen, he or she is already "in." So Catholic, baptized non-Catholic, and unbaptized catechumen share at least a sense of membership together in the body of Christ.

The recruitment and timing of stages present real challenges for some creative genius. The Black Catholic parishes in Washington, D.C., have little problem in rounding up ten or twenty non-Catholics a year for inquiry classes. If evangelization and the apostolic nature of every Christian's call were emphasized in the homilies and in adult religious education, any parish could seemingly find a few who are interested in becoming Catholic without ruffling ecumenical feathers and plucking Christians from other churches to join the Catholic Church.

It is an indictment against our confusion or our getting fat and lazy that we cannot increase our adult population by five percent a year. Maybe we have been talking too much to one another during and since Vatican II in an attempt to get our houses in order and draw up some pastoral plan of renewal together for our own implementation and edification. If we are celebrating the Eucharist every Sunday with lectors, commentators, leaders of song, choirs, extraordinary ministers, altar ministers, permanent deacons, and celebrants, if the Gospel is being preached, if works of mercy are being performed and works of justice pursued, if even a few are really praying, then certainly we have some good news to share!

The timing of the stages is the toughest part for pioneers in the new Rite to implement. Persons interested in becoming Catholic have a right to know when the initial conversion-journey begins and when it ends in conversion to Jesus Christ in His Church. They ought to know as well how much will be expected of them. Such information can be difficult to give if we take into account the freedom of parish affiliation in our cities and suburbs. Often the first thing a prospective convert wants to know is why it takes a year in your parish and only five months in a neighboring parish to become a Catholic. It does not reflect well on the Church if you advertise "the most up-to-date approach" or "a first-class treatment of issues." It is cheap to talk about cheap grace.

So we are treading lightly. First we went from five

months to nine months, and then to a year with a month off in August because of heat and vacations. We pushed our recruitment beginning with Holy Week and through the Easter season since that is a good time to reach those who have thought about joining a church and those Catholics who are looking for more from their practice of religion. Beginning the precatechumenate toward the end of May before most parochial operations close for the summer gives the catechist June, July, and two or three sessions in September for this first stage. Entrance into the catechumenate occurs in the third or fourth Sunday of September, and election and postbaptismal catechesis follow the liturgical year. Pentecost closes the cycle in late May or early June, and you are ready to begin again.

It sounds neat and rather clear—except for one thing. The guts of the entire process is short-circuited in a twelve-month cycle. Our experience is that the catechumenate proper may take twelve months by itself and that the precatechumenate could easily fill six months. Our eye is trained on a two-year cycle, but the suggestion of such a period brings an outcry from those who desire to participate fully in the sacraments more quickly than in eighteen months. And then the pressure that results from being among the few parishes that have instituted the catechumenate grows, and the merit badges of being part of a twelve-month process get waved in the face of the catechist and the priest. So the time for large-scale implementation of the initiation rite is here if for no other reason than that those who feel the need to go to an eighteen- or twenty-four-month cycle need the rest of the parishes to be doing at least a twelve-month process.

And the need for a longer process is not from stupidity or ignorance. It has nothing to do with race or economic status. It has solely to do with allowing enough time for conversion to take place and for convictions to be formed, old ways unlearned, and the fruits of contemporary scholarship shared with masses of people who want to know what they believe and why. The whole dynamism of the initiatory process is lost if what was missed is offered in a postgraduate course. It is silly to make up ground by offering the entree after the dessert.

What we are feeling in Saints Paul and Augustine parish in Washington, D.C., is what architects of the Rite view as normative and what historians point to as the earliest practice of the Church. There are enough personal experiences to be had, enough catechesis to be covered, enough praying to be done to consume a two-to-three-year cycle!

Just as the Rite itself is flexible and elastic, so this book comes with a restrained plea: to those who can, read the Rite four times, pray over it, try it, and join the debate over the best ways to implement it. To those who have cash, resources, and expertise, spend them on studies of how it is being implemented across the country. Use some of these resources to develop materials for a program and a number of working sessions for people already busy in the field. And would it be Catholic if we did not ask the bishops who have had some experience with the new Rite of Christian Initiation of Adults to assist those involved in this ministry with some careful and flexible direction as well as with a mandate for its gradual introduction into the parishes of this country? Let us go slowly, but *let us go* in a process of trying it on for size, making improvements, and gaining experience.

First Stage:
The Precatechumenate

A Time of Welcome

THE first phase of the process of Christian initiation is now called the *precatechumenate*. The "pre" prefix gives a clear note that whatever happens here is a prerequisite for what follows.

The catechist is responsible during this phase for introducing the individuals who have found their way to the catechumenate to one another and, as importantly, for enabling the local parish community to introduce itself to these prospective catechumens. This is the time for hospitality and informal meeting, a time for story telling, for first impressions that can set a tone for the total process. The catechist presents the whole array of the local parish to the group after the group is comfortable with itself.

Obviously, the catechist has the opportunity to present only those who are alike in thinking and taste. Another way to go would be to present the entire spectrum of parish membership from most radical to most fundamentalist. The catechist's potential for presenting his or her image of the local parish is practically unlimited. I think it important to present as diverse a picture of the local parish as possible.

Before that presentation, however, the group must feel as "at home" as possible. The room, refreshments, seating arrangement—all should give the impression of being close to one another yet businesslike in a relaxed way.

Hospitality at this stage is crucial, and arrangements should avoid any kind of classroom atmosphere.

Those who have come together will have some

writing to do, so place a table or group of tables in a rectangle or a circle. Allow for only as many places as you expect persons to fill them.

It is amazing what a rug on the floor can do for a room to bring folks around a table together and (pet peeve) what decent seating instead of tan metal folding chairs can do for lengthy discussions! Hot tea, coffee, or Sanka and plain iced water (for the noncaffeine addicted) also add a lot to the sessions.

In any case, meaningful introductions and impression-sharing usually occur at the beverage table. We toyed with the idea of a bar but rejected it. We want folks to remember what they discussed the next day! In fact a rectangular or circular bar-type setup is not a bad idea for the catechist working with the precatechumenate. The catechist sits at the bar with everyone else, relaxed and involved in the process rather than seeming to be the instructor.

Breaking the Silence: The First Meeting

WHAT is the catechist's role?

The catechist is the silence breaker. The first challenge is to get the group to "open up." There are a host of gimmicks and techniques for doing this, some of which you may find helpful.

Being big believers in first impressions, we have attempted to steer clear of using a lot of sophisticated introductory procedures. Everyone in the room presumably wants to tell or deepen his or her own life story, or express personal insights about religion and God. Those who want to become Catholic and those Catholics who may have been recruited to review the basics of faith are there not to stop smoking or to fill in their income tax forms. They are there to meet the Lord, and they are usually predisposed to receive the catechist and the message. Elaborate simulations or techniques at this point are usually confusing.

We have had success in breaking the first silence by creating the silence of filling in a form. Everybody expects a form at the beginning of things, and it can be useful in helping the individual meet himself or herself. The form ought to be the catechist's creation, incorporating basic information needed for record keeping but enhanced by original questions that help the individual focus on who he/she is, why here, how he/she got here, what he/she would be doing if not here. The information can give the catechist invaluable help from the start in determining individual capacities and differences.

In communities where there may be illiteracy, the catechist should have two or three persons at hand to assist those who may have difficulty. Some of the Apostles might have had a very difficult time had Jesus passed out a form to be filled out before receiving the call.

Here is the latest form we have used:

Saints Paul and Augustine Parish
Precatechumenate   **Introduction**

Hi! A lot of people feel a little awkward when they meet a group of strangers, especially when they are asked to introduce themselves. This sheet will help us to get to know one another and to remember important things about yourself that you may want to share. Everyone has a name. Write your first, middle, and family names:

(First)   (Middle)   (Family)

Your maiden name, if applicable:_____

Your mother's full name *before* she married: _____

Your father's name: _____

What city and state/country is your birthplace?

When were you born? Month____Day____ Year ____

How many sisters? _____Brothers?_____

Did your parents ever have you christened or baptized? _____

Where, if you remember? _____

Have you ever been a full-fledged member of another Church?_____

Church name_____ Where?_____

Did you go to Sunday school or Bible school?_____

Did you ever go to a parochial school?_____ Name of school _____Where?_____

Are you married? _____If yes, to whom? _____
Children? _____How many children? _____
Names of children: _____
_____
What elementary school did you attend? _____
High school? _____ College? _____
Where? _____
What major and minor? _____
Where do you live? _____
Home phone _____
If you had $20.00 and five hours free tonight, what would you do?

_____

_____

_____

Who is the one person most responsible for your being here?

_____

We have about 60-70 hours of discussion, sharing, studying, living, and praying to do together. When is the best day and time during your week for a two-hour session?

(Day) _____ (Time)
_____
What is the worst time for you? _____
Are you employed? _____ Where? _____
Work phone? _____Do you like what you do? _____
What is your favorite television program? _____
What radio stations do you listen to? _____
How often do you read a newspaper? _____
What is the last book you read? _____

We end the form with three thought questions. You can probably do better than these, but they work for us.

1. What picture or idea of God did you have in the

first grade? Do you have now?
2. What is the difference, if any, between God and
Jesus?
3. Is there anyone living for whom you would be
willing to die?

And that is a good place to begin the discussion.
The person who can give his or her name and picture
of God now has given the catechist more than enough
for the first session. Having the group sketch on
chalkboard their pictures and images of God opens
the members up to one another in a way that has
never failed to be lively and real.

You watch the reactions of the group to one another
as they speak. You see persons coming together "out
loud," and place the onus of the conversion journey
from the very beginning on the persons who are going
to have to make some weighty decisions along the way
in the months to come.

Need it be said that the catechist at this point is
totally nonjudgmental? The object of the first session
of the series of introductions is not to react negatively
or overreact positively to the images and ideas presented but rather to see just where the individuals are.

After a short break, the catechist should try to get
the difference, if any, in the minds of the group
between God and Jesus. Though this can be frustrat-
ing for catechists trained in Scripture, the usual
tendency to represent or image Jesus of Nazareth as
"Superman" ought to be "on the table" from the
beginning. The catechist should record all these pictures and images for the group and for self for later
use. It is this host of images that will be confronted
directly in the catechumenate phase. To know these

images "from the jump" is to know one of the biggest parts of the catechetical enterprise for this particular group of people.

Before the first two-hour session concludes, the catechist has three details to cover: collecting the forms, setting a permanent day and time for meeting, and assigning the group some reading. This can easily be done in ten minutes, but try to reach a consensus on the best day and time and to arrange alternatives for those who find them impossible. Sifting through the forms in front of the group gives the catechist a chance to comment to each of the persons about favorite television shows or radio stations and sets up a relaxed personal relationship between catechist and group.

We have had great success in using the handy book, *Now That You Are A Catholic* by Father John Kenney, C.S.P. (Paulist Press). Before we leave the first meeting, we give each member a copy with a short reading assignment. The reason for using this book now is simple but at the core is the focus of the revised Rite. People setting out on a journey in Catholic life are in a very specific parish with a group of persons whom they have begun to know. They are in the midst of a community of Christians whom they want to know better. One of the best ways to get to know the Catholic community and what it is about is to see it in action. And the book answers some of the more obvious questions people ask about Catholic life and practice. Before the first session ends, it is a good idea to let the inquirers ask questions they might have about Catholic faith-life. As a general introduction to the externals of Catholic life, *Now That You Are A Catholic* helps clarify for the inquirer what will be the primary concern of the precatechumenate: Who is this parish, how did we get here, what do we believe, why do we think you are important, what makes us the same as and different from the next parish over or from Catholics in Tanzania or Brazil or the Philippines?

There may be many "stumbling blocks" to be removed for inquirers before they are invited to attend any liturgy in the parish. But they should be encouraged to familiarize themselves with the various activities or societies in the parish. Parishioners may be contacted to invite the inquirers to attend one or other meeting of such societies so that they will come to know the parish in some depth. The first session might close on this note: "You are welcome! We want you to know us better. We want to know you."

After the First Meeting

To dispel quickly the notion that the revised Rite of initiation is a series of inquiry classes and to plant the seed that the process is one of incorporation into a living association of believers, schedule as many different persons who exercise key functions in the parish to speak at different meetings of the precatechumenate. If the cycle of your process is one year with three months allotted to the precatechumenate, then at nine or ten meetings have a different person from the parish family give a brief explanation of who he or she is and what he or she does. With a question and answer period, you can easily use forty-five minutes to an hour of a two-hour session. Putting the "members of the family" on first gets your group to the sessions on time since they do not want to miss the announced attraction. These portions also add life to the catechist's ongoing explanations in the second hour of the kinds of things the parish does and the rationale for liturgy, social action, religious education, fundraising, and socializing.

A word about special guests is in order. Everyone wants to meet the pastor whether the catechist thinks so or not. For the pastor to take on a flesh-and-blood identity early in the catechumenate can be helpful to him and to the prospective members of the community which he serves. Such things as where he is from, why he became a priest, what experiences he had had before becoming pastor, what kind of family he has are usually more enlightening to the longtime parishioner than to the non-Catholic. For the newcomer, however, the opportunity for a personal introduction to the pastor fixes him quite clearly as a member of the human race, an important function and status for those afraid of or suspicious about priests.

Even in a team ministry, the person responsible for management and administration can provide enough description of duties that relate to the group's experiences of balancing checkbooks and surviving in an inflation economy, making clear parallels between running a parish and a home. One of the best sessions we ever had featured a co-pastor who used to pay the bills and centered on ways he tried to give creditors the impression he was paying them when he did not have enough on hand at the time to cover what was owed! But that perhaps could be the substance of another book.

The chairperson or president of the parish council is an obvious person to introduce. One of his or her functions should be to conduct "the election" of these candidates to membership. This "election" is celebrated by the ordinary or his delegate on the first Sunday of Lent. For this reason the parish council and chairperson ought to get to know the catechumenal candidates well from the very beginning.

The description of the method of choosing the parish council, its organization, its work and concerns can be an eye-opener to Catholic and non-Catholic alike. Unfold this information not by tedious notetaking but in a personal chat, a heart-to-heart talk by one of your co-worshipers who has been chosen from the pews to assure that the parish is acting in concert with all and for the good of all.

Religious (men and women) who are part of the parish staff should have a spokesperson to explain their lifestyle, which includes vows and rules as well as the various functions they may perform in the parish. Assuming that Catholics know the origin of religious communities is a mistake. Explaining the symbol of life consecrated under vows can enrich the meaning of Christian initiation.

The heads of two or three functioning parish organizations should be invited to introduce themselves and the work in which they are involved. An invitation likewise to the leader of a defunct or near-defunct group can set that person thinking about his or her responsibilities. Using the catechumenate to resurrect a lifeless parish is definitely a goal of those who have redesigned the Rite.

Anyone joining a parish is ready to respond to a presentation by a young person who can speak to the difference faith can make in growing up. A teenager or young adult who can speak of the value to them of persons who share faith-life with them can go a long way in convincing the doubting Thomas!

I am not sure that it is wise at this point in the process to introduce representatives of various Catholic movements. There will be time during the mystagogy stage to meet charismatics, encountered couples, cursillistas, and others. It is the family of faith, the local parish, that will initiate these potential Christians and not a diocesan, national, or international movement. There are enough differences in approach among the leadership of a parish for the future member to absorb without going outside these functions to other groups which the parish may support.

When these introductions have been made, the other half of the precatechumenal sessions is a similar kind of personal introduction to the religious practices and traditions of Catholics and the parish. Many converts come to the Church through participation in novenas or seeing and reciting the rosary. The historical development of these prayer forms or other such practices should be explained.

It takes a good hour and a half to explain the different artifacts in the church building, and it takes more, if the stained glass windows tell a story. It is amazing how many Catholics walk past a statue of the Infant of Prague without a thought as to where that devotion originated. Whether or not you are a devotee of the Infant, you can be sure a non-Catholic wants an explanation—and deserves one.

Holy water, the Sign of the Cross, Stations of the Cross, vestments, vessels, other statues, kneelers, tabernacle, altar facing the people, old main altars, side altars, sacramentaries, lectionaries—all need explanation. Have your group taste unconsecrated bread and wine. Burn and explain incense. Visit reconciliation rooms and confessionals. Celebrate a dry run of the Eucharist over two or three sessions. Like it or not, the missalette or hymnal ought to be explained so that new members do not become slaves to the printed word, "reading the Mass" to follow the priest. Depending on circumstances, and if it is not premature, the precatechumate may be an ideal time to celebrate Scripture with the group, as preparation for their being introduced to participating in the Liturgy of the Word.

This *tour de force* achieves some amazing results for both catechist and longterm Catholics in the group. The advent of reconciliation rooms brought welcome relief to anyone who had to explain the confessional box. Try as I could, I was never able to convey a sense of Christ working in those acoustically walled cells. Even to how the priest opened and shut the little doors and could not see the penitent seemed more an exercise in forced anonymity than in healing and forgiveness. And the light on the penitent's side went out automatically when the contrite of heart knelt before the closed door. There were more reactions and questions about that electrical process than about any preliminary explanation of the power of binding and loosing. My four-year experience with the cate-chumenate led to the inevitable conclusion that the confessionals would not be missed if anonymity could be provided. They are gone in our church, and we make only passing reference to their presence in other churches.

If your parish church still has the lovely marble or wood altar of the shrine variety, it gives the catechist a concrete fixture to develop an introductory history of the liturgy. The priest facing the altar which faced the wall and reading in Latin gives a sense of both how far we have come in intelligibility and in restoring the sense of Eucharist as well as of what we may have lost. My thought is that the sense of adoration, of wonder at the active but mysterious presence of the Lord in the action of the Eucharist is, for many, a potent factor in their decision to become Catholic. The study of different emphases in the celebration of the Eucharist can lead to a balanced eucharistic spirituality if per-sonal prayer before the tabernacle is discussed.

The presence of Catholics in the catechumenate leads to a fairly in-depth discussion of these precate-chumenate areas and to a valuable sharing of the Catholic transition which really began with Pius X and early reception of Communion. If you can recruit some sixty- and seventy-year-old Catholics to your catechumenate, you have the resources for some personal faith experience from another day that can provide the non-Catholic with an invaluable sense of

Catholic culture of the past and its earlier practices, a living measure of where we were and where we are. And the long term Catholic adds a living element of the creative tension in the Church between the "new" and the "old." That tension *is* present in the Church, and not to have it present in the catechumenate is to create and present an unrealistic picture of the Church.

It has been a rewarding experience to recruit for the order of catechumenate a coordinator who appreciates the "new" after worshiping according to a Latin ritual in a clerically dominated Church. To let her or him reflect out loud from time to time on the changes in the Church gives a grass-roots flavor to topics that could be dry as dust.

The coordinator should keep the attendance records, show an interest in all, and not be afraid to pick up the phone to find out how folks are doing and why they may have been absent from the last session. Our coordinator is a true "den mother," looking after the material and spiritual needs of all in the group and providing a running report of the activities or situations of the missing.

While treating of "old and new," the liberal-conservative, progressive-reactionary duality in the Church should be introduced in the precatechumenate. If the parish sells both *The Register* and *The National Catholic Reporter,* unsold copies provide living proof of two palpably different approaches to Catholicism. Reading what Catholics publish can improve the perception of the catechumen that the Catholic Church is an umbrella organism. The umbrella is the Creed, and under the umbrella fit the most diverse political, economic, and theological minds as well as the most diverse forms of spiritualities and cultures.

If one country can count as Catholics William F. Buckley, Jr., Senator Edward M. Kennedy, and Dorothy Day, you cannot deny the variety. Or if the Gallo brothers and Cesar Chavez both communicate at the Eucharist, you may wonder what makes for consistency in the Church. But you cannot help but appreciate the diversity of persons who claim allegiance to Christ in the Catholic communion. It is no surprise that social activists see the Church as one of the last institutions in our society wherein changes can occur through an appeal to a common faith.

The Local Parish

THE tangible ways by which the local church celebrates the Gospel way of Jesus Christ would not be complete without a serious treatment of the history of the parish. Here again parishioners who have been around before the catechists or the priests can be most helpful.

Why tell the history of Saints Paul and Augustine— or any parish? The faith into which the inquirer is seeking initiation is one, holy, catholic, and apostolic. But the revised Rite of Christian Initiation of Adults places the greatest importance for leading initiates along the journey of conversion on the personal involvement of sponsors, catechists, parishioners, and priests in the local community of faith. It is *this* parish family that is incorporating the interested parties into its flesh and blood. It is *this* parish family that will form and inform the catechumen in every aspect of faith in Jesus and in day-to-day living out of that commitment. To skip over the history of *this* parish is to avoid the very dynamisms that root the parish in the Catholic tradition.

Our parish has an awkward name. To name a parish after two saints who lived a couple of centuries apart indicates at least a merger of parishes. How did the merger happen? Well, you see, Saint Paul's Church was built on the edge of what used to be the city limits of Washington in the District of Columbia. And Saint Augustine's was a parish that grew out of a chapel named after the then Blessed Martin de Porres. Saint Augustine's was developed by Black Catholics for

Black Catholics and, at one time, was the only church for Black Catholics in the city. That is surely important to the descendants of those who built Saint Augustine's. It ought to be important to any predominantly Black group of interested non-Catholics who come to inquire about becoming a Catholic Christian.

Once we introduce the Black-white background of this parish, we owe our listeners the whole truth. And the whole truth is that Saint Paul's parish was a creature of its time in at least one respect. It kept Black Catholics in the back of its church building. The priests at Saint Paul's had developed the knack not only of referring emergency calls from Blacks to Saint Augustine's but also of discouraging Black Catholics from attending Saint Paul's. There are stories to fill a book of refusals to give Communion to Blacks at Saint Paul's and of insults repeatedly added to injury.

The startling fact is how Black Catholics, abused by white Catholics, not only kept the faith but also grew in members and gradually deepened the quality of faith-life. From Saint Augustine's parish came the leadership of many of the parishes integrated by Cardinal O'Boyle when he became the first resident archbishop in Washington, D.C. And the numbers of converts to the Church from Saint Augustine's parish—in fact the number of converts from most Black parishes in Washington—puts the white Catholic parishes to shame.

It comes to us as no surprise that Black Catholic parishes around the country are taking the lead in implementing the revised Rite of Christian Initiation of Adults. In spite of the abuses of institutional racism the Black Catholic parishes have no shame in inviting their brothers and sisters to taste and see the goodness of the Lord in the Catholic Church. And still they come, even when the cynics question why anyone would want to become affiliated with an organized Church, much less with a Church that insulted and persecuted Black people in this generation.

And, friends, we now worship in that church building from which we were excluded twenty and more years ago. They say crooked highways come from crooked politics. The same could be said of crooked parish names. But for some mysterious reason, the Lord makes the crooked way straight for those who want to find Him in the Catholic parish named after Augustine and Paul.

Not to cover that history for our inquirers (and readers) is to miss the importance of the struggle and the contribution of Black Catholics to the Church in Washington, D.C. The Church is divine but also human—all too human in many cases. And no statement or declaration finally made a difference. The difference, the survival, the vindication of faith was made in the Church that is now begging Black Catholics to take leadership, to get involved in parish councils, to become priests and religious sisters and brothers.

If you should want to join us, come to us with your eyes wide open. You heard the story here first, in the beginning, before you finalized any decision to go deeper into the way of Jesus. The history of the Church as a human institution is, sadly, the history of the country which protected the rights of slaveholders for two hundred years and which is struggling to redeem that sin today. The history of the Church gives more than sufficient witness to the need for continual reform. But it is the truth. That the reforming Church is always being reformed is not necessarily a comfortable thought for many. But it is the truth.

The glorious truth is that the parents and grandparents of our congregation put their faith on the line with their lives and, while taking caring of their own, rattled the institutional Church to the point of its making radical changes. Are you gutsy enough to join a parish that recognizes its need continually to reform and to contribute to the reform of the whole Church in the process? It is a good question—and a real choice. And it is not restricted to the single parish of Saints Paul and Augustine.

The Choice

As mentioned earlier, our experience at Saints Paul
and Augustine is of a one-year cycle from the beginning of the precatechumenate (first phase) to the
formal ending of the mystagogia (fourth phase). Since
nothing of import happens in sultry Washington during August, we take a break in that month, but it is a
very important break. During that break the non-
Catholics are going to decide on whether or not they
want to become members of the parish, that is, catechumens, and those who staff the catechumenate are
going to assess the interest and intensity of those
seeking membership.

It is here that the future undoubtedly holds some
change for us. When thinking of an eighteen-, a
twenty-four-, or even a thirty-six-month cycle, this
point between precatechumenate and catechumenate
becomes crucial. It is crucial enough in the twelve-
month cycle. The concerns are these: has the prospective catechumen met self, the local church, and
Jesus to the degree that he or she is ready to see,
hear, and feel more? Has the local church developed a
meaningful membership program for the catechumen-
to-be so that the lengthy catechumenate proper is
accomplished with a feeling on the part of the catechumens that they are "on the inside looking out"
instead of vice versa? Finally, is the revised Rite
sufficiently attuned to the American phenomenon of
numbers of already baptized Christians seeking an
experience of initiation which parallels the process of
the Rite but also fully respects the dignity of the

Baptism in Christ which has already been celebrated?

These are big questions, and the answers will be developed in parish after parish over the next decade. From our limited perspective we offer a few suggestions. Distribute a list of questions as you bring your precatechumenate to a close. Here is a list of questions that we have used with some success, but only after we discussed fully the meaning of the *questions,* not the answers.

Questions to Ponder Before Becoming a Catechumen

1. Do I feel that God is working in Jesus reconciling the world to Himself?
2. Do I feel that Christ can be known and experienced in the various sacraments (Baptism, Confirmation, Eucharist, Reconciliation, Matrimony, Holy Orders, Anointing of the Sick)?
3. Am I ready to admit that I need others to help me to become me *fully?* Does this recognition of need for others extend to my relationship with Jesus Christ? Do I want to be associated with other believers to grow to full stature in Christ?
4. Can I become convinced that Jesus "washed my sins away," that I am free from all evils (my own included) and from final death?
5. Is the Saints Paul and Augustine community of faith ready for me? Do I like what I see here? Am I ready for Saints Paul and Augustine? Can I find Jesus here? Am I ready for the whole Church?
6. Am I ready to see that life in Christ is a constant process of growth and change? Am I ready to make some changes in my life to keep in touch with the

spirit of Jesus? Can I be a growth agent in the Catholic Church by helping to keep the Church in touch with Jesus?

7. Can I be part of a Church that has had a racist as well as humanitarian history? Do I believe that I can serve the cause of good by overcoming evil, even evil within the Church?

8. Do I believe that Jesus can be found in the rich and poor, in the social outcasts, the beggar, the junkie, the wino? Can folks who cannot read or write show me a face of the Lord?

Then, to see where the individual is, schedule a one-on-one interview between catechist and prospective catechumen for an in-depth personal assessment of readiness for membership in the Church. The catechist should fall over himself or herself in emphasizing the freedom that is present. There is no pressure. Personal conversation about such a possible decision can reveal to the catechist both the readiness and dispositions of the seeker to become a member. If the desire is there but the commitment to the local community of faith or to a willingness to explore the message and activity of Jesus is unformed, the person might be invited to put off a decision at this point. Instead of pressuring, ease the transition to the catechumenate phase of the program by encouraging the person to become an inquirer. This status could be celebrated liturgically or merely understood, depending on the need of the person (RCIA, 12).

A point of caution. When using a more individualized approach such as is described here, several catechists may be needed in the catechumenate. A spiritual counselor and/or director of the catechumenate often do a better job at this interview. Leaving the critical decision as to whether a person should defer a decision to become a member of the Church is a big responsibility for a single catechist to bear.

For the one whose attendance, interest, and desire are both alive and expressed, the decision to become a catechumen is one that should be made privately with the catechist and celebrated publicly with the parish community, preferably at a Sunday Eucharist. At this decision point a sponsor or sponsors should be identified, for their active assistance begins in the catechumenate proper.

Role of Sponsors

SPONSORS or godparents, as the Rite indicates, should be Catholics who have more than a passing awareness of the challenge of the Gospel as well as a degree of involvement in a local parish, particularly and preferably *this* parish. If the sponsor knows the potential catechumen beforehand, a lot of preliminary "getting-to-know-you" can be obviated. If the person seems ready for membership but knows few Catholics, then some of the Catholics involved in the catechumenate process for their own growth and renewal can certainly become sponsors. Sponsors who are not part of the catechumenate process should be encouraged to become affiliated in some way. Unless the mature Catholic sponsor has been active in adult religious education in the last ten years, he/she is sure to experience the phenomenon of student outdistancing teacher in very short order *(RCIA,* 19, 43).

The choice of sponsor should be at least ratified if not approved by the catechist and the priest involved with the order of catechumens. The catechumen has the right to open and free access to a mature, stable, and committed Catholic who will be required during the coming months to share his or her faith with the catechumen in a most intimate way. The Rite calls for sponsors along with the whole community to help the candidate "learn to pray to God more easily, to witness to the faith, to be constant in the expectation of Christ in all things, to follow supernatural inspiration in their deeds, and to exercise charity toward neighbors to the point of self-renunciation" *(RCIA,*

19). That is not an exact picture of everyone who currently practices the faith. Yet there are more such people present in our parishes than many of us want to believe, and we owe them an opportunity to minister to our new brothers and sisters *(RCIA,* 43).

While speaking of rights, we point out that directors of the catechumenate owe sponsors individual and/or collective sessions. These meetings can include shared prayer for their ministry, for their catechumens, and for the work of the parish and the Church. These "side sessions" should not be the responsibility of the catechist alone. They should produce open and honest assessments of both candidates and sponsors. The catechist could profitably preview and review the work of the catechumenate with the sponsors, using them as a sounding board while catching up with those sponsors who may have been forced to miss some sessions.

Catechists themselves need formation. They have a right to as much help as they can get. The director of the catechumenate must be certain that catechists perceive the importance of Scripture as part of their own prayer life as well as of liturgy as the heart of their apostolate. Ongoing courses in Catholic teaching may be provided for adults in the home parish or on an inter-parish or diocesan level. Ideally, special training programs for catechists should be developed and made easily and conveniently available on any one of these levels. Catechists must be especially aware that adults do not learn as children do but must be involved in discussing, reacting, and researching as they enter more deeply into the verities of Catholic faith. At the same time the catechist helps the catechumen to grow in knowing what Catholics believe and live. He/she must be a prayer leader and good celebrant in group liturgies and be able to prepare catechumens themselves for this kind of ministry.

If possible the director of the catechumenate should see that the catechist has the assistance of a spiritual advisor to be available as candidates approach the point of deciding to become Catholics. Wise and enlightened direction by one experienced in faith development should be provided in the parish catechumenate. Such spiritual guidance should, in fact, accompany the candidate throughout the catechumenate. Steps must be taken, decisions made, in the very important journey to becoming a Catholic.

Important to realize is that the whole parish is catechist. We need to build communities of faith. Fr. James Dunning observes, "The RCIA gives us an entry point and a reason to begin building communities of faith. It calls for small groups who meet with the catechumen to share stories, questions, prayer and faith. These groups are called the 'catechists.' "[3]

[3] "The Rite of Christian Initiation of Adults: Model of Adult Growth," James B. Dunning, *Worship*, Vol. 153, No. 2, March 1979, p. 149.

Beginning Members

THE problem of the local parish developing a method of helping the catechumen feel like a beginning member has to have more to it than the right to Catholic burial and to receive monthly envelopes. Here the Church in America is going to have to put some substance on the Roman ritual. My guess is that more than half of those who approach the Church for membership have already received Christian Baptism. The remainder who are unbaptized may know more about the power of faith in Jesus Christ and the vast potential of the Church to minister to its own and the world than some of our best "dues-paying" Catholics. Generally we do not find ourselves dealing with converts from tribal deities, but rather with persons for whom Jesus is a familiar figure. It seems perfectly consonant with the spirit of the Rite to invite catechumens to become active members of parish organizations and projects from the point of their catechumenal consecration. How else can they learn the works of mercy and justice and the work of the parish unless they are involved in some weekly aspect of parish life?

The new Rite creates troublesome situations for those who have been in inquiry work as well as for those who are trying to move from the inquiry approach and gradually implement various aspects of the Rite. One is the time it takes to get to that Easter Vigil celebration. This situation is intensified by the catechumens themselves who want to celebrate the Eucharist fully and yet know how much more they need to know and experience before they will feel comfortable "talking shop" with Catholics. It would relax a lot of pressure and help to develop a two- or three-year cycle more readily if the catechumen feels a part of the family from the beginning of the catechumenate phase and if that feeling grows as the catechumenate progresses.

Let me pose a possibility that we have not tried, and then await the thunderclap from those trained in these areas. For those who have been baptized in a Christian church and who have expressed a desire to celebrate Eucharist fully, why not fulfill their desire? After a suitable period of eucharistic catechesis and with clear understanding that the fullness of membership has not even been achieved, could we not parallel these already baptized with the youngster who has reached the age of reason and approaches the table of the Lord? This proposal goes against the liturgical opinion conclusion that Baptism-Confirmation-Eucharist are, in that order, the sacraments of initiation. But we seem, as a Church, to be violating that ideal while a resolution is nowhere in sight.

If we followed this compromise, out of respect for the Baptism of the potential convert and in keeping with our practice since Pius X, we could ease any pressure on the already baptized catechumen and the catechist, and we could more readily construct an eighteen- to thirty-sixth-month cyle that really did the job of preparing new Catholics to contribute to a revitalized Church. The climax of the process could be the confirming in the Spirit that has already been experienced.

The alternative is to develop a rite for the incorporation of the already baptized into the life of the Church. Perhaps this task is a project for today's liturgists and sacramental theologians to sink their teeth into and meet another real need for an apostolic Church. This situation has no parallels in the Church of the Acts of the Apostles, and a satisfactory solution has yet to be proposed.

Pardon that digression. We return from our August break and continue the precatechumenate for two or three sessions until a Sunday in late September when at a principal Eucharist we consecrate our catechumens.

Summing Up

THE precatechumenate phase is clearly a time of meeting between the prospective convert and the local community. Thus the value of having members of the parish involved in the catechumenate process becomes clear. It is a time when the catechumen is introduced to what we do as a parish, and that introduction can be threatening to those parishes that have not implemented the directives and the suggestions of Vatican II and the diocese. Thankfully, many parishes have made the transition from those days when parishioners merely attended church to when parishioners *are* the Church. There is no substitute for seeing and hearing parishioners pray, share their faith, and plan and implement the Gospel. No one individual, be he or she priest or lay person, can tell it all to the catechumen. No one individual alone can be presumptuous enough to be the basis upon which an interested individual can decide for or against membership in the local church.

The key to the change from convert classes to the process of the revised Rite of Christian Initiation of Adults is the participation of the whole local assembly and its representatives in the formation of the new Catholic. Initiation is preeminently a parish family affair in which catechist, coordinator, and catechumenate staff are agents of that local community. Aidan Kavanagh has stated that this Rite provides structures "that do not merely assume personal and corporate *renewal* but require it." He says it may be "explosive on the pastoral level."[4]

The first explosion, radical break, or transition from old to new occurs in this precatechumenate phase when the parish assumes the formative role in the lives of those to be initiated. And the parish as a family with a council should decide that it wants to exercise its apostolic ministry by setting up a catechumenate not as a parish program but as the constitutive element of its parish life. A clear conclusion is that the erection of a catechumenate process is as ongoing in the life of the parish as is the celebration of the Eucharist.

The parish, after reviewing its corporate life in its council or other deliberative bodies, may decide not to set up a catechumenate until it puts its house in order. Surely the demands of the precatechumenate are such that if you have a parish in disarray, it is not ready to introduce a nonmember to membership. Some parishes would do well to emulate certain religious communities who, a few years ago, stopped receiving new members until they had reorganized their constitutions and practices and brought themselves up-to-date in the life of the Church. What a refreshing breeze of candor were a parish council to say to themselves and the parish that we are taking no new members for a year until we implement a pastoral plan that incorporates Church renewal in liturgy, religious education, parish council organization, and works of social justice!

We did this once in another area, and the benefits were enormous. We were supporting a program of Saturday religious education that used volunteers from outside the parish to teach C.C.D. to children not in our school. Any honest assessment of the program led to the inescapable conclusion that it was not religious education but a creative play period.

Deciding that parents could play with their own children, we placed resources in the hands of the parents and introduced four community organizations that began from children who used to come to Saturday school sessions meeting in their own neighborhoods. Parents and other interested community leaders went beyond the religious "play period" to construct year-round programs of educational and cultural enrichment.

The next year saw the demand for sacramental preparation on the part of parents who were recruited to organize a true Sunday school program. They were trained and, from their own need, created a program that resulted in the hiring of a director of religious education.

The purposefulness and the warmth of the precatechumenate must come from a parish that knows itself and is confident enough to open itself to new members without fear. That is not to say that any parish is a spotless lamb. The Lord is the one without sin. The parish and its catechumenate are of a pilgrim nature, of a journey in faith, redeemed sinners all and sure in the saving power of Christ. The precatechumenate is the parish's way of introducing itself.

[4] Aidan Kavanagh, O.S.B., "The Norm of Baptism," *Worship*, Vol. 48, No. 3, p. 145.

Second Stage:
The Catechumenate

The Celebration

THE transition from precatechumenate to catechumenate results from a decision, a decision which is
celebrated in the revised Rite of Christian Initiation.
While every decision to enter upon a new stage in the
process is mutual, resting with local church and
candidate, the decision to become a catechumen falls
more heavily on the catechumen. The next decision,
to elect the catechumen to the immediate preparation
phase of purification and enlightenment, will involve
assessment and reflection more on the part of the
parish and its representatives engaged in the initiatory
process.

The rite of becoming catechumens includes reception of the candidates, the Liturgy of the Word, and
prayers. It may be followed by a Eucharist. Depending
upon circumstances, the catechumens, sponsors, and
catechists ordinarily leave after the Liturgy of the
Word. What takes place is clearly a celebration of a
parish ready to welcome candidates and happy to have
the opportunity to minister to persons who desire the
fullness of faith. Normally, as indicated, the personal
interview between catechist and catechumen has an-
swered any questions and relieved any personal anxi-
eties of the potential catechumen. Those who choose
not to become catechumens are nevertheless invited
to the celebration, and they are incorporated formally
into the process whenever they make their decision.

The sponsors and the Catholics involved in the
catechumenate participate directly in the decision
celebration. We make it clear in the liturgy who is

Catholic and who is not, for the Catholics are not prayed over or anointed. The sponsors, having normally met the other candidates and those involved prior to the celebration, are introduced to the parish assembly at this celebration as co-ministers with the total parish in this journey in faith. They leave with the catechumens after the Liturgy of the Word, and the rite of becoming catechumens is completed. They start ministering to the catechumens at once. The empty seats in the church are a powerful sign of the community of faith that gathers together and opens itself to newcomers.

Remember that this journey in faith is for the parish as much as for the individual catechumen. Stories and discussions from the catechumenate should find their way into the homilies of priests in the parish and in other meetings of adults as both essential to the parish involvement in the process and contributory to parish insight into the growth in faith process which should be part of parish life.

The tone of our Sunday liturgies involving the catechumens is of a studied informality and friendliness. The ease with which catechist or coordinator introduces those who have decided to become catechumens and their sponsors should be matched by the personal warmth and friendliness of a celebrant who, from the precatechumenate experience, knows everyone directly involved in the liturgy. Try to think of the last time you read this kind of description in a Roman ritual:

> The celebrant greets the candidates in a friendly manner. He speaks to them, their sponsors and all present pointing out the joy and happiness of the Church (RCIA, 74).

68

And how can we be friendly, joyful, and happy in a
glum, read-from-the-book liturgy? We need celebrants
who can smile without being Cheshire cats to make
this liturgical event a joyful experience for the whole
people.

The introductory dialogue can be made much more
personal than simply asking and answering questions
from a printed page. It should be personal to the
catechumen if it is to be meaningful to the whole
congregation. It takes remarkably little time for the
candidates to prepare their own statement of why they
want to become catechumens instead of simply answering "eternal life" to a standardized question.
There is no confusion at all if the priest has met with
the candidates individually during the decision-mak-
ing process and can phrase questions that go to the
heart of their prior conversation. There may even be a
point made in the conversation that the catechist or
the priest thinks the congregation should hear. It is no
disservice to the ritual to ask the catechumens to
repeat that point. We find it particularly valuable to
have the candidates state publicly a privately held
hope that they want the support of those who are
already Catholic in coming to know the Lord and how
to serve Him. There is nothing quite like a little nudge
to the faithful from the newest in the community.

The most important effect on the parish is to have
these catechumens assume an identity, and their
answers to these initial questions, easily audible
throughout the church at a Sunday Eucharist, can
arouse interest in the persons in the pews to go out of
their way to meet the new catechumens, either at a
reception or simply on the front steps of the church
after the Eucharist.

The first promise (RCIA, 76) gives the celebrant

leeway to include particular references to individual catechumens. The candidates' readiness is indicated, and there follows one of the most serious questions in the Rite, the importance of which cannot be left simply to the question itself but to the sincere preparation of the total congregation to welcome these candidates and to be guides on their journey in faith. The question is put to the sponsors and the entire assembly: Are you ready to help (these candidates) come to know and follow Christ? If the answer ("We are") is perfunctory and empty, this liturgy is meaningless. The process does not simply work by its own mysterious power or in a passive way. The parish must know as they accept these new members that their own reason for living out the Gospel is now enriched by their free decision to take responsibility for the formation of new Christians.

A signing of the cross on the forehead and the senses follows. In our case, we have omitted the signing of the senses and have asked the sponsors and the whole parish present to sign each of the catechumens on the forehead. This signing can be more readily done if the candidates have been facing the congregation and the celebrant.

Word of God and Minor Exorcisms

THERE are a series of celebrations of the Word of God and of minor exorcisms provided during the catechumenate phase after this celebration. The anointing with the oil of catechumens may be anticipated (*RCIA*, 103), and we have done so at the signing with the cross at this first reception. The celebrant signs and consecrates with the oil, and the sponsors and congregation simply sign with the thumb. The congregation understand the anointing with the oil of catechumens when used at this point, and the catechumens appreciate a sign of the cross that is an anointing, especially if they have already been making the sign of the cross during the precatechumenate.

The readings for the Sunday liturgy follow this introductory dialogue and signing. The effectiveness of using readings assigned to the day and emphasizing the quality of faith and commitment on the part of catechumen and parish is helpful. As the Rite is introduced, we have found it worthwhile to extract from the assigned readings what is normally there in terms of communal support in the faith process. Those who like to pick readings are free to do so. The homily content should be self-explanatory and reflect the friendliness and joy of the introductory dialogue. The role of God's Word in the formation process concludes the homily. We, the Church, are the descendants of that early Church that composed the New Testament under God's inspiration, and, as inheritors, we are servants of that Word that has been revealed to us. It is a great sign if the catechist and a sponsor have proclaimed the Word as lectors in this celebration.

Then the catechumens are presented with Bibles to be their constant companions during their days of catechumenate. Celebrant or catechist can conduct this reception. The catechumens have been nourished, on the bread of the Word.

We omit the Creed since the presentation of the Scripture implies faith in the Word of God. Those already Catholic may need to be enlightened on this. An invitation to Catholics to participate in Scripture study programs can be neatly included at this time or before the Eucharist concludes. The Rite also suggests a presentation of a cross at this point, which can be more than just a gift idea for sponsors and those already Catholic in the catechumenate.

The prayer for the catechumens (RCIA, 94) is modeled on the General Intercessions, and if the Rite is celebrated during a Sunday Eucharist, the General Intercessions can easily include petitions for the catechumens, their sponsors, and the congregation's ministry to the catechumens.

Here at Saints Paul and Augustine parish we do not invite the catechumens to leave before the celebration of the Eucharist but rather to stay, since exclusion, however traditional in the life of the Church, simply is not comprehensible to our catechumens or congregation, not after such a welcome. Catechumens understand that they are not to receive Communion until their Baptism or reception.

Since our catechumens come from Christian backgrounds, we omit all reference to pagan religions and forswearing false religions. There are areas in this country where allegiance to other non-Christian religions should be taken into account. For some former devotees of astrology as a religion, we could consider a reference to a renunciation of stars and planets as controlling personal destiny. Celebrations of the Word, exorcisms, and blessings of the catechumens in the Rite provide types of prayer services to be celebrated in the sessions and in periodic Sunday liturgies with catechumens and sponsors present in places of honor.

Catechist and priest celebrant are given more than adequate direction and resources for the first stages and for the various steps of the catechumenate. Freedom of choice is left to pastoral considerations and planning based on the needs of the catechumens and the desire to celebrate progress and growth. The same freedom may be exercised in the content of the catechumenate sessions, and the order which follows, designed for our parish, may not suit your needs. It is an outline of areas which, we have concluded, must be treated to assist both the catechumen and the Catholic to mature in true faith. It is ideal if the areas covered weekly can be related to the themes of Sunday liturgies and celebrated occasionally as the various stages of this phase of the catechumenate.

It should be obvious by now that what goes on in the sessions is not kept there but rather is brought into the liturgies of the whole parish. We meet one night a week for two hours or more, and as we go deeper and deeper into the faith experience of Christians and our Jewish ancestors, the history comes alive in the discussions and prayer of the catechumenate. We cheat those Catholics not directly involved in the process when we keep what goes on in the catechumenate a secret from them. To explain an Old Testament reading or a Gospel with anecdotes from the catechumenate is to make that Scripture come alive in terms of something going on in your parish right now. The presence of Jesus Christ in the Word of God is still vastly underrated in most parochial celebrations. Sharing feelings and insights of catechumens and those already Catholic on Scripture and its interpretations with the whole parish can enrich the communal appreciation of the Bible. Is it too much to hope that the implementation of the revised Rite, with its emphasis on involvement of the entire parish, will lead Catholics to appreciate the Word of God as a distinctive presence of God in their lives?

If the power of God's Word to transform life, to make for personal conversion, and to strengthen and heal the whole parish can be appreciated by the persons in the pews, then the celebration of the Word in the parish can be an introduction to Catholics praying the Scripture in common, as the Liturgy of the Hours suggests. Until now, the bulk of the Catholic community has felt religiously "cheated" if they cannot eat and drink at the Lord's table. They have come to recognize in recent times that God's Word is nourishment. It is bread for the Christian life.

The shared catechumenal process has shown us the unique power of sharing God's Word and its meaning in our lives, and catechumens come to know the unique presence of the Lord in the Scripture as a presence that is as special as it is different from His presence in the Eucharist or the other sacraments. Thus, the potential of this Rite to assist a parish in basing their spirituality on the Word of God can be realized in the manner of cross fertilization, where the contributions of the catechumen to a deeper understanding of and feeling for the Word vastly enriches the catechesis of the pastor or the catechist and is shared by the whole parish.

Catechesis: The Atmosphere

ONE of the more underdeveloped notions in current Catholic practice is understanding the role of the catechist. We have spoken of the capacity of the catechist to break the silence in the precatechumenate. Here in the catechumenate stage the most important function of the catechist is to create the atmosphere for God to do His saving work. After scads of training sessions and after a variety of new series of textbooks for elementary and high schools, we seem still to be bogged down in the content and/or methods approach to catechetics. The liberal-conservative polemic, the book-burners who want a return to the "old-time religion," the psychologists who fall over themselves on strategies of method and approach—all have made the catechist the equivalent of a troubled teacher. In speaking with lay catechists, you sense with all too many the insecurity that comes from being pulled apart by all segments of the Catholic community.

Lay catechists are fair game for any workshop or training program more from their experience of insecurity in conveying the Word than from their need to grow in conviction and faith in the Lord. Because of this insecurity (which is largely the work of some catechetical entrepreneurs), many Catholics are very reluctant to become involved in the ministry of catechesis to the young and have a blatant fear to minister to their peers the saving message of Christ.

The person who believes in Christ and in the mission of the Church to spread the news that salvation can be found in Christ and that His kingdom is near to those who believe can be an apt person to develop into a catechist. Certain personality traits are also desirable, such as a willingness to allow people to reveal themselves and courage to be unafraid of the momentary reversal when the whole group seems to have left you or, worse, to be against you. The catechist of adults has to be willing to be misunderstood for a while if the resolution of the misunderstanding or the growth of the catechumen needs time.

We will go into the content of the catechumenate as we have developed it, but it must be repeated almost to nausea that content transferred simply from notes or from a page of the Bible to the intellect of the catechumen is neither the goal of the process nor the work of catechesis. Information conveyed in the catechumenate is for formation in faith. It is information that will lead to convictions and that comes from testing those convictions in the life of the catechist.

The catechist, then, is one who is sensitive to the needs of the individual catechumen, one who knows when the individual is making a contrary point from personal misunderstanding or from insufficiency of self-appreciation. The catechist knows the difference between that personal insecurity which may manifest itself in silence or compulsive speaking and that true self-analysis marking moments of growth in understanding and feeling. The catechist is first a fellow traveler on the journey in faith and has to earn the role of guide by winning the respect of the catechumens through a slow, sometimes painful, process of sharing personal sorrows and joys in the light of Gospel faith.

Part of the sensitivity to the individual includes respect for the experience as well as the education of the catechumens. If the group runs the gamut from

semiliterates to Ph.D.'s, the catechist has the happy
obligation to make them all feel at home in much the
same way as Jesus appealed to the unlettered fishermen and the learned of His day. This task challenges
those who have studied books more than experiences. The value our society places on higher education and denies to the wisdom of age or to the
experience of the poor and disenfranchised is in direct
contrast to what we can conclude constituted the
appeal of Jesus' personality and message. It becomes
quickly evident to the catechist that the mastery of
concepts and ideas takes a decided second place to
willingness to be taken over by the person of Jesus
and to become friendly with the personalities in the
biblical story of faith. Understanding Jesus is a by-
product of the process; incorporation into His values
and His death-resurrection is the goal. And that
experience is without parallel in the classroom experiences in most American colleges and universities.

We continually have to remind ourselves of the
fairly grimy lifestyle of early fishermen as well as of
their wisdom about nature's calms and storms and the
failure of the sea to deliver up fish sometimes when
people need them most. It is a healthy exercise in
making the directness of Jesus' appeal real to those
who are lost in the thicket of the Passion narratives or
in wondering about the truth of the Old Testament
miracles. The catechist's sensitivity to head, heart, and
feelings of the catechumens should not scare persons
away from this ministry. Saintliness is not required as a
qualification to catechize. Sinners who are conscious
of their sins and the Lord's forgiveness can make the
best catechists.

Since the revised Rite of Christian Initiation of
Adults is totally integrated with the liturgy, the cate-

chist's awareness of the liturgical readings and prayers in the three-year cycle is important. To convey the ancient understanding of God dealing with a people more than with individuals, of His relationship with a nation, a tribe, a family and their worship of Him as a community is as important now as when we first started talking "communal" prayer twenty years ago. The Church as a people who worships God, who announces a kingdom that is universal in appeal if not in membership, has to know what it is to be part of a community at prayer. And the catechist is a liturgical minister of that understanding of the prayer of the people. Without that appreciation of God making a people His own through the covenant relationship, and of the people realizing His presence and celebrating it as a people, our Eucharists and other prayers of the Church will inevitably be done together because of convenience to people and celebrant and not because we are a priestly people, saved *as* a people.

The experiences of Black people coming to realize their identity in the country of their oppressors and struggling to bring their heritage to new birth have given us an appropriate parallel to this sensitivity to the biblical "people of God" theme that has had a difficult time taking hold in the spirituality of our parishes. Madison Avenue advertisers and Hollywood television and film producers seem to have discovered the key in programming to a Black *people* and to the American *people* more than the Church's ministers have. Most Church programs and services today are designed for groups of young or old, marrieds or singles, engaged or college students. Yet the parish *is* the assembly of the *whole* people, and this key reality of a people's life and worship can be experienced only in the assembly of *all* the groups in a parish. The catechist's awareness that we are a people descended from those "nobodies" whom God made into a nation and freed from slavery in Egypt, that we are descended from a people who murdered the prophets, that we are the inheritors of a people who went to jail, to the lions, to the stake as well as to worship can lead the catechumens into a sense of worship as a people that has yet to become normative for most parishes.

Sensitivity to liturgy and to personal prayer forms can make the catechumenate a school of prayer. Forms of meditation, of shared prayer, of using Scripture and liturgy to develop patterns of personal prayer can gradually be introduced to the catechumens as part of the weekly sessions. One of the most refreshing experiences of the catechumenate is hearing again that simple request, "Teach me to pray. I do not know how to pray." Obviously the catechist should be at home in a couple of forms of prayer and be able to distinquish technique from the essence of prayer.

Finally, and most critical to all that follows, there is the catechist's sense of Scripture as the revelation of God in and through the experiences of real persons and His people. If any prerequisites are to be spelled out for so important a ministry as that of catechist, the study of the development of the Bible must head the list. True, many of those who followed Jesus lacked the scientific grasp of recent archeological discoveries, language study, history, and awareness of pagan stories that influenced a good part of the Scripture. Yet their grasp of what God had done for them was reinforced by the culture of their times and by learning their "family history"—from the patriarchs and Moses through the prophets and the Exile—from "their mother's knee." Our culture is not supportive of those family and religious roots. Our rationalism and attempt to erase everything from the past that cannot be "proved" have rendered the Bible unsophisticated to some and devoid of credibility to others.

The situation is further complicated by the constant exposure of the religiously inclined to self-styled preachers and healers on radio and television who seem simply to have opened the Bible and developed their own explanation of certain texts with an authority that is intimidating to many. The popularity of the Oral Roberts, Billy Graham, or Reverend Ike approach to the Bible does not argue for its inclusion in that form in the catechumenate process. Vatican Council II and the major self-renewal effort of the Church in these days involve sharing the fruits of our awakened appreciation of the Scripture with the catechumens and the whole parish. The Bible is not a magic formula for worldly success or sure healing from ailments. There is not a biblical hero or heroine who has grown rich off God's revelation and lived to enjoy those riches.

There are some preachers and healers who prey on the hopes and the distress of the poor while pocketing people's hard-earned money in return for spiritual favors. They must be confronted in the catechumenate process especially among open-minded people hungering for the Word. For that experience of religion is one that is all too familiar even if never embraced by the catechumens. The literal interpretation of Scripture as preached and taught by the untrained can lead to serious crisis and even loss of faith when pain or misfortune strikes those who thought that right living would surely lead to painless life here and hereafter. That we can hold both the

crucifix and the jeweled cross of victory before catechumens is a bonus for us and a stumbling block to
those who would make religion a palliative for every
personal ill.

The catechist has to have studied and appreciated
the cultures of the various stages of the Scripture, or
else the points of those Scriptures will be lost in the
lack of conformity between cultures. The literal interpretation of the Bible leads only to gross misunderstanding and to a quotation for every condition
imaginable. Literalism and fundamentalism also rob
the catechumen of the invaluable experience of being
part of the process of growth in faith that is the
development of both the Old and the New
Testaments.

The catechist, then, should have studied in depth
the Pentateuch, the Deuteronomic history, the Prophets major and minor, the Psalms, and the Wisdom
literature. The history of Israel is basic to that content
development as is the history of Israel's enemies and
friends. The study of the Synoptic Gospels, of John's
Gospel and Revelation, of the Acts of the Apostles,
and of the Letters of Paul is also integral to a catechist
in the catechumenate. For a catechist there is no
substitute for true knowledge of Scripture.

That knowledge of Scripture cannot be left at the
simple scientific awareness of how the Scriptures
came to be or what an individual sacred author is
talking about or attacking. For after the balloons of
ignorance are popped, after *The Jerome Biblical Commentary* and *The New American Bible* have become
worn in the study, the catechist has the unenviable job
of translating this information into her or his own
personal spiritual formation before considering the
catechetical ministry. The student of the Scriptures

who cannot use the acquired knowledge in renewing her or his personal spirituality has missed the point—that all this information is for Christian formation. How many of us who suffered during endless hours of study of literary forms and archeological digs never made the transition from classroom, to chapel, to life!

After the catechist understands all of Scripture, she or he must realize that the calling is to tell the story again. Like the watchmaker who can successfully repair and replace all the broken pieces, the catechist analyzes the stories, to the limits of personal under-standing as a believer, in order to make those stories part of her or his own life story. This step is but the latest chapter in God's story of saving us. The catechist studies the stories to be the best possible storyteller in an age when the only storytellers left are the classic comedians. Truth is still stranger than fiction, and the story that needs telling in the catechumenate is a collection of narratives spanning centuries told by a variety of tellers, all of whom the catechist needs to know somewhat intimately.

The catechumen, meanwhile, cannot have his or her progress really measured by conventional classroom testing. Absorbing the point of the story and the spirit of faith in the Scripture is ever so much more important than mastery of details. The catechist knows the details to contribute to the telling of the story. The catechist must convey the feeling of God's presence and how the faith of the individual grows. And that is the genius of the catechetical experience: telling and hearing the stories deepen faith at both ends of the process. Sometimes the roles of storyteller and "audi-ence" get reversed, and the students end up "telling it like it is." That is the best sign of a good catechumen-ate. Everyone gets the spirit of the story and can unfold its different aspects to one another.

Here is an aside based on what we know about the multi-leveled development of the written Gospel from what was preached and remembered about Jesus: I think it possible to compare the catechumenal process with those groups of early Christians who met to review what Matthew or Mark or Luke had written and to add their own remembrances to those first written drafts of what are our canonical Gospels.

I like to picture for my catechumens those who walked and talked with Jesus adding an insight or correcting a saying of the Lord for the young scribe working with Matthew's draft. Part of the process during my catechumenate storytelling time is to bring such reflections alive. The conversation is always sparked by the observations of those committed persons gathered around the table with me. Like the early Gospel community we, too, are threatened by an unbelieving generation. Like them our hearts also burn within us as we enter more and more into the living message of salvation in Christ which is the heart of the Good News.

The reactions of catechumens to storytelling is inspiring. One story recalls another, until the recollections and remembrances of their own stories of faith-experiences are a compelling witness of the power of God in the lives of the catechumens on their journey in faith-life. For me such occasions have been spirit and new life.

Catechesis: An Outline

INEVITABLY, what follows will be taken by some as the meat and potatoes of the revised Rite of Christian Initiation of Adults. You can hear some religious educators saying, "Surely the content of what is to be taught in the catechumenate is the difference from the instructional classes of the past." Our experience is that this is true only to a degree. What is much more important is seeing the whole parish at work, the development of a formative process for the catechumens, the sense of joining a community that is active in all its members, and the enlivening of the liturgical experience of Lent and Easter.

The content outline, in fact, is drawn from the ritual, not mandated by it. Aware that they are writing for a variety of Catholic churches and parishes, the Sacred Congregation for Divine Worship has left content schemas to the prudent judgment of catechists, pastors, and parishes. So this outline is our own configuration of stories, facts, and acceptable interpretations, served up in a purposely incomplete fashion since we are always changing and adding pieces and counting on current events and the dynamics of each catechumenate grouping to enliven and alter the content.

To answer that favorite clerical question asked in religious bookstores "What do you use for converts?" makes us pause. We use Catholic Book Publishing Company's paperbound edition of *The New American Bible* (Saint Joseph Edition, 1970). The large type is readable, and the "How to Read Your Bible" and "The Lands of the Bible" (historical survey) sections are very helpful to the catechumen. By the time the catechumenate concludes, the newly baptized usually need a hardbound edition because the less expensive edition has a way of falling apart after much use and exposure to one Washington summer and winter. But it works.

Strictly as a supplement to the Bible but primarily for sacraments and morality, we have had success with *An Introduction to the Faith of Catholics,* by Reverend Richard Chilson, C.S.P., newly revised and expanded (Paulist Press, 1975). It is three hundred pages but easy reading in most sections. Its value for our situation, in which we combine already baptized Catholics with baptized non-Catholics and bona fide catechumens, is in its revised sections addressed in italics to the pre-Vatican II Catholics. Father Chilson clearly indicates that those sections may be skipped by non-Catholics or read later, and we so direct our non-Catholics. Generally all find the book at least helpful as a short supplement to our Bible study and an adequate presentation of sacramental and moral theology.

There are an ever-increasing number of other books in the field that may be more to your liking. The norm for selection should be the catechist's ease and familiarity with the resources to be used. This book, *A Journey in Faith,* is *not* designed for use by a catechumenate. It is for planners and implementers of the restored process of Christian initiation.

We begin the catechumenate (or end the precatechumenate) with a reading of the first three chapters of Ephesians or the first two and a half chapters of Colossians. The reading from Ephesians concerns the mystery of salvation and of the Church. Paul's prayer (Eph. 3:14-21) is a beautiful and meaningful welcome to those undertaking their spiritual journey. The letter to the Colossians (1;2:1-15) is a stirring introduction to the Christian life, centering the catechumen's attention on Christ, the central figure in God's saving work. We select for attention those early sermons in the Acts of the Apostles, in order to enter into the faith of the early Church just after the Resurrection.

Then we fix the Jesus of history in His time and place, careful from the beginning to date His birth as correctly as possible in 4 or 5 B.C., before the death of old Herod. The dating game of B.C. and A.D. is reason enough to set the limits on our Jewish-Christian faith story. It should be liberating to the beginning catechumen to know that from today to Jesus' birth is 2000 years and that from Jesus' birth to the tribal traditions about Abraham is close to 2000 years—a total of 4000 years in a history of humans that may run from 3.2 to 3.7 million years. Given that history, this revelation of God is a relatively recent development. This date fixing takes the Bible off the hook of having to explain everything that ever happened to every human being and lays a foundation for understanding Scripture as the story of a faith developed through experiences of God's revelation in the life-story of people, from Abraham to the eyewitnesses of Jesus.

The Christ who is preached and the conversion and Baptism that are required of the early believers are both the core of the kerygma and the reason that these catechumens are present. The kerygma—the apostolic proclamation of salvation through Jesus Christ—refers repeatedly to the fulfillment of a longing and an earlier covenant or promised relationship.

That reference takes us in the first session to the Passover-Sinai event of the thirteenth century B.C. Moses shares the wide screen with Jesus. And in our setting at Saints Paul and Augustine parish we find it natural to push back to Exodus 1:8 and the slavery the new king in Egypt began. We are descendants of two peoples enslaved, the first by North Africans, the second by Europeans.

The first Passover and journey to freedom and the Promised Land, with the call of Moses and the plagues, the great escape, the desire to return to slavery, the quail and the manna in the desert, the water from the rock, the covenant at Sinai, the golden calf, the death of Moses, and the entrance into the Promised Land are material enough for countless stories. We try to deal in two sessions with this Exodus-Sinai event as the backdrop of Jesus' constant references and as the key to Old Testament faith. There are stories of faith here that can absorb attention for weeks, but we are limited by time.

Covenant relationship and the laws of the period regarding such covenants need explanation, as does this personal experience of Yahweh and Moses and the reasons for belief. We treat of the natural explanations for the successful escape through the Sea of Reeds, of the quail, and of the manna. We show how the inspired authors saw what we may see as wonderful coincidence in the light of the larger plan of Yahweh to save and be with His people as slowly He forms them into His own during their desert experience. Only after dealing with the Exodus-Sinai event are we ready to introduce the notions that are elementary to a contextual interpretation of the Scriptures.

Literary Form

Washington, D.C. is the place to study the concept of literary form. Surely every high school and college course in Scripture explores this fundamental key to the interpretation of the different books of the Bible.

But religious programming on the parish level, in the media and the pulpit, has not reached the great numbers of older Catholics or of many attracted to the faith with any ideas relative to this basic principle of understanding the Bible. We think that one of the greatest ministries we perform in the catechumenate is to assist the community of faith in "getting into" the mind of the author of any book of the Bible. It is amazing how little history and culture need to be developed beforehand but how much background is requested after the most preliminary concepts of literary form are presented.

The reason Washington is a great place to talk about literary form is that we are the home of so many literary forms. The press release from Senator X or President Y denying complicity in evil is a literary form ignored by citizens of the District of Columbia, who have come to trust only personal appearances of political leaders where people can "see their eyes." The *Washington Post* had two distinctive literary forms on the same page on the Watergate story: the reportage of Woodward and Bernstein (*All the President's Men*) and the "official" White House reaction to the break-in.

Any newspaper, in fact, is ideal to introduce the concept of literary form. News reports, interpretative reporting, editorials, political cartoons, comics, sports, society, weather forecasts, advertisements, and horoscopes are enough different literary form examples to overwhelm the beginner. These examples can make the point quite clearly that the Bible must be treated with at least the same respect as the daily newspaper. Not to do so may lead to utter confusion and complete misunderstanding of the message. Comics and hard news have to be read differently.

Then the question of truth surfaces. There is a true-to-life relationship between reality and the comics, or we would not respond with a laugh. Something in Peanuts arouses the response "Yes, that's what I'm like" or "I have been there before." How often a novel holds our attention because the author's genius makes true-to-life characters express something incredibly deep about human vulnerability or the power of love.

So many catechumens come to us with a complete background in soap operas and other television series that we can profitably use such shows as well as their commericals to illustrate literary forms such as love stories, adventure yarns, and comedic situations.

The literary forms that surround us parallel the literary forms of the Scriptures. The fact that most of the letters of Paul were not originally letters but sermons or pamphlets does not take away from the presence of letters. There is history in the Bible, such as the books of Joshua, Judges, Samuel, and Kings. There is faith presented as history in books like Daniel and Deuteronomy. There is national legislation presented as history and as coming directly from God in Leviticus and Numbers, embodying a long tradition, reflected much earlier and much later, that the leaders and legislators somehow shared in the work of God. The divine right of kings and the conviction that God gave the New World to Europeans as a gift may, in retrospect, make a mockery of God's will. But the conviction that God is "on our side" is older than the Hebrews. It takes the latter prophets and Jesus to reveal that God is on the side of all His creation and that He does not take sides except between the faithless and the faithful.

Only when the catechumen is comfortable with the

variety of literary forms in the Scripture can we proceed. To know poetry, history, allegory, fiction, adaptation from pagan myths, preaching (Gospel), apocalyptic family stories, plays, and prophetic writings and to be able to acknowledge that God uses human authors to speak His revelation is to slide easily into the world of the Bible. To sense the truth of creative fiction, the truth of Shakespeare or Langston Hughes, is to arrive at a readiness level to perceive the truth of the many-faceted Scripture.

Alex Haley's *Roots* has done as much for the study of the Scripture as for forging the ties of heritage between American and African Blacks. His priceless popularization of the training of young warriors in the tribal history has contributed to our understanding of how the stories of forefathers centuries before are transmitted with accuracy to the children almost as part of the price of becoming adult. The craze to find one's roots simply by tracing ancestry is to miss the "stuff" of ancestor history. The substance of tribal heritage is in the stories of the family or tribe who survived against all odds or who developed a culture that makes our fast-food, collapsible, disposable culture seem barbaric. Haley' *Roots* and the exposition of King Tutankhamen's world in Washington's National Gallery of Art gave us more than enough resources to appreciate the way stories and traditions developed and how they contribute to one's rootedness. They helped us also to value realistically and imagine creatively that all that has gone before has not necessarily been primitive in the negative sense.

To know family history and to take legitimate pride in one's origins is a fascinating way to enter the Bible as a story of stories that is our own. It also puts the lie to those preachers and teachers who do not respect the nature of the Scriptures and the intents of the authors of various books. To forget the preoccupations and intent of their writing is to fail to respect the faith of the Church that has always attempted to revere how God acts through inspiration, prophets, and saints.

Big Question: Evil

The question that never fails to start and maintain discussion is the hardy perennial for philosophers and theologians as well as for those who know the meaning of suffering. If there is a good God, how do we account for evil in the world? The question is a natural for discussion, but more importantly, it places the guts of the faith question almost at the beginning of the process. The Exodus-Sinai event and the context of Jesus in the story of salvation helps the catechist to get more readily to the problems of evil posed by the more learned settlers of the Promised Land. It becomes clear that God alone is the Author of Life. Evil negates life and cannot have its source in Him. Faith in the one true God signals Him as the Deliverer from all evil. Until Israel came to such faith, firmly and undeniably, evil would dog their footsteps. Appeal to a multiplicity of gods would not liberate them.

Belief in more than one God was clearly a conviction of the earlier Hebrews, and their God, Yahweh, had been introduced to some as the greatest of the gods. Polytheism among the Hebrews plus the active belief of their Canaanite neighbors in their false gods made it clear that a belief in Yahweh as the one only God was to be the ground of faith of the true Israelite. This faith was taken together with what Yahweh had achieved in delivering them from slavery, sin, and certain death. And the answer to the Big Question about evil in the world could not involve Yahweh in the causing of evil, for He is the God of the living. The story of Genesis, of the creation and the fall, is best understood if one's questions and the questions of the authors of Genesis chapters 1-11 are similar. The problem of evil and a conviction about the power of a good God is at the heart of the faith process.

The introduction of the theories of authorship, the Priestly and the Yahwist editors, is helpful in analyzing the two stories of creation. The dates of authorship do not negate the power of the stories to speak to faith's conviction that God wants good and not evil for creation and creatures. Rather, the relatively late dates of the writing of these stories can show the growth in faith that was characteristic of the Israelite nation.

The two stories of creation (Genesis 1:1-2:4a and 2:4b-2:25) provide the classic faith answer to the problem of evil. God made everything good and in love made the gifts of creation to humans. The Fall makes it clear that God's only "mistake" was the gift of freedom to humans—a forgivable "mistake" because the divine intention was not to create puppets on a string but reflections of the divine freedom.

The story of the fall of Adam and Eve is important for its description of personal freedom gone awry and of the social and cosmic consequences of evil. The lure of knowing evil and not being satisfied with good is the story of teenagers growing up and adults thinking the "grass looks greener" on the other side. The consequences to a family when one of its members gets into real trouble (evil) are well known to families in our parish. The consequences of leaders' countenancing devious means to obtain more power which, in turn, results in their fall from power are not a distant memory. It was an everpresent reality to the people of Israel as well. This piling up of evil upon evil creates a climate of cynicism and betrayal and a depressing sense of everything falling apart. Many current events are graphically illustrated in the multiplication of evil from Adam and Eve to the Cain and Abel fratricide to the quest for superiority and becoming like God that are embodied in the Babel story.

It is common for us to spend four sessions in this early Genesis material both for the theology and for the reality of the good and evil stories. Sometimes we can easily switch to another expression of the battle between good and evil as pictured in the Book of Job. The attractiveness of Job to persons who feel as though God is testing them with evil in spite of their goodness adds another dimension to the faith process: everything, even resistance to evil, is a gift. The failure of either story to solve everyone's problems completely, like Bufferin for headache, is a healthy and helpful lead into the ambiguities of the history of Israel. The importance of the covenanted relationship is not that every question has an immediately satisfactory answer. Faith-journey is filled with deserts, with desire to return to slavery, with longing to give up one's freedom and go back to the fleshpots; and the catechumens who know life recognize that Job and Cain and Abel are not corny creations but typical of real life. God is good, and the only conceivable reason for God's tolerance of evil is His reluctance to compromise the gift of freedom.

Family History

The patriarchal stories of Abraham, Isaac, and Jacob are the written versions of stories that had been passed on orally through generations of Hebrews. The faith experience of Abraham's conversion to Yahweh and his change of lifestyle give the opportunity to reflect on the characteristics of religious experiences and theophanies in the Old Testament. Dream books abound in sections of our parish, and any number of people have faith in dream interpretation that is as powerful as it is superstitious. But the interpretation of dreams in the Old Testament is as revelatory of God's designs as are the experiences of Moses on Sinai or the crossing of the Sea of Reeds. The difference between the contemporary practice of dream interpretation and the experiences of learning God's will in the Old Testament is evident in the results.

The stories of the dreams of the Old Testament that led to the preliminary images of the Lord as interested in Abraham's family (tribe) and the promise of descendants as numerous as the stars are committed to writing only after the stability of the kingdom is established. The very establishment of the learned and priestly societies in the time of Solomon is taken as the fulfillment of those promises of a firmly rooted people made centuries before. Dreams that turn into a nation are dreams that possess a power.

The stories of Abraham, Issac, and Jacob are stories that are written in the light of their fulfillment in the deliverance from Egypt. For their true effect, they ought to be studied in the context of the great Sinai covenant. They illuminate and clarify the identity of the Hebrew people. The conviction of Abraham that God was asking him to return his gift of a son, the character development of Esau and Jacob, the behavior of Joseph and his brothers—all reflect a primitive morality as well as a picture of persons struggling with faith and life. These narratives are family history stories, and they are of the essence of real life, not of some idealized society or heavenly kingdom.

The taste of the Old Testament for immediate rewards from God and a lack of belief in an afterlife make the faith of the Old Testament patriarchs and prophets even more intriguing. The biggest problem we consistently have with the Book of Genesis is not the creation and fall or their literary forms. It is not even the picture of Abraham about to sacrifice Isaac. It is the unfairness of the apparent blessing and inheritance that Rebecca and Jacob steal from Esau. That inheritance lost without the possibility of rescue in an afterlife makes the deceit and trickery all the more reprehensible.

It is clearly not a story written to show God's fairness. It is a story that shows that the human institution of the inheritance is more powerful than fairness. God's tolerance of duplicity here is no more or no less to be wondered at than the "mistake" of freedom that led to the emergence of the sorry state of original evil or sin. God allows even evil to permit the plan for salvation to advance, the salvation of a people in time and with tangible, temporal results. What are more tangible than the end of slavery and the birth of a free nation?

Let us digress here to point out that the study of the Old Testament by catechumens provides an opportunity to witness the way we have spiritualized God's saving work, not always to either our advantage or to God's. While eternal life and resurrection do revolutionize the faith-life, the terms of salvation should not become so totally spiritual as to become ethereal. The satisfaction of working to establish the kingdom in time has its share of temporal and tangible reward. The works of faith make for personal joy, and the power of petitionary prayer to satisfy needs for the sake of the kingdom should be stressed.

The whole work of social justice as embodied in the Old Testament is to make clear to all that creation is not to be hell but rather a foretaste of the joy of the kingdom of heaven. To express salvation in terms of real-life freedoms and the fulfillment of life's promise, and to subdue the forces of nature for the benefit of all is to begin the important work of seeing salvation and redemption in this-worldly as well as next-worldly terms.

You now have a picture of our handling of the Genesis material that indicates the fun we have in exploring our religious folklore with an eye to the quality and the kind of faith of our forebears. The traditions they tell are signs of their growth in faith, eminently suited to the parallel process of the catechumenate. A review of Exodus and Sinai and the stylized entry of the chosen people into the Promised Land places those critical events in the perspective of a national history.

The Book of Deuteronomy is treated in much the same fashion as John's Gospel: a serious theological interpretation of all that has occurred with a view toward institutionalizing and regularizing the faith content and perspectives of the early believers. With Deuteronomy comes the exposition of the importance of the Law as the mediation of God's will expressed in the covenant.

The thesis of the Deuteronomist is that God is faithful to the covenant and that those faithful to His Law will find their rewards. This thesis is illustrated in the Deuteronomic history of Joshua, Judges, Samuel and Kings. The Book of Ruth, while not technically part of that history, gives a short dramatic playlet on the rewards of faithfulness. It introduces a theme that is appropriate to later prophetic writings and the New Testament, a theme especially suited to converts. The theme is that the faithful woman, permitted no legal identity in the culture of that period and the foreigner as well, can share in the promises of the covenant. This happens through allegiance to Yahweh and His Law. We use the Book of Ruth as the first short serial that was designed to build anticipation with more than enough surprises for a four-part drama.

We find the time to present in context all this material that older Catholics had in Bible history and Protestants know so well. To do so is to discover the true human spirit in all the positives and negatives that make us love and hate ourselves, yet with a significant difference from the study of secular history. This real history, chronicled by those who lived it or shortly thereafter, is filled with details of love, power-seeking, pioneer spirit, and superstition that in the hands of a true storyteller can show how constant human nature is across time, country, and race.

The overshadowing presence of the Lord, the constant reference to His Law and power, the way faith in Him fills the void of the barren wife and exalts the lowly to high places are part of a faith history that continues into the New Testament. Not to find time to treat this material is to deprive catechumens of the way their ancestors lived and believed. These narratives are not "nice stories" or "dirty books" that can be treated or not depending on interest. They are the *I Remember Mama* and the *Father Knows Best* stories of faith.

To ignore Yahweh's story is to ignore how and why we have come to live and pray and believe as we do. To treat these stories out of context is to miss the covenant history and promise of which we are the inheritors.

The David material and the obvious conflict between the nomads and those who were settlers comprise an important turning point in faith history that should certainly take a session. For as much value as there is in settling in, building a temple, and erecting a kingdom in the parishes of our own day and in the days of our grandparents, so, too, there can be the loss of feeling for the fact that we are a pilgrim people. We travel freely on this earth unencumbered by the cares of the world or of earthly security.

If the imagery of the conflict between the Hatfields and the McCoys is helpful, use it. In the West the farmer and the cowboy took a long time to become friends. So in Israel. Those who followed David into the construction of a permanent kingdom recognized that they ran the risk of losing touch with their Father Abraham, who was a wandering Aramaean. The picture of Jesus, the itinerant preacher of God's kingdom, and of priests, Pharisees, and Sadducees who lived in and around the Temple area of Jerusalem enjoying the status of the institutionalized "church" of their day comes all too quickly to mind. The occupational hazards of placing too much trust in the institution and too little in Yahweh are there in the tension between nomads and settlers in David's time.

And what is with us today? The occupational hazards of institutionalized religion and a faith that has settled down to build fences and houses of worship and schools and chanceries and so on may be the core of a lack of vision. Perhaps we do not see or hear our apostolic vocation and the consequent demand that we preach the Word and incorporate new members in the faith community, whether we are popular or unpopular. The cutting edge of this apostolic drive to seek out the lost and preach to those who have not heard has come from those corners of the Church where the pipes leak or where there are no pipes because there are no buildings.

God's Fidelity

After the glory of Solomon, God's fidelity and Israel's responses are in marked contrast and even in conflict. The collapse of the Northern Kingdom is laid to the inconstancy of that kingdom. The role of the prophet is that of spokesperson for the Lord and the in-house reminder to the king of the requirements of faith-living. The prophetic movement is one unparalleled in other nations built on some kind of faith. For these divinely called prophets had to pay for their unpopular stands for faith and Yahweh against false and superstitious worship and the failure of people to deal adequately with the needs of widows, orphans, and aliens. The prophets are to become models for the faithful Jew and the committed Christian.

Without going into detail here, we like to study the personalities and writings of the four major prophets and a few of the minor prophets like Hosea, Amos, and Micah. If possible, they should be discussed as the movement of history progresses. The fall of the North brings little insecurity to the South. The prejudice of the Jerusalem Jew against the Samaritan on grounds of orthodoxy is only heightened, and a conviction develops in Jerusalem that "it can't happen here." That it does happen in keeping with the prediction of the prophets has led to an understanding of prophets as persons who could read the future. There reading of the future, as a matter of fact, was based directly on their reading of the present. Future destruction would occur if true faith in the Lord and fidelity to His covenant were not restored.

Josiah's reform in the seventh century gives a breather to the self-destructive process. More important, it affords the Scripture writers the chance to put a final form on the Pentateuch. Josiah's reform is not enough to save the Southern Kingdom from the power of its enemies. What is most evident to the band of prophets loyal to Yahweh is this: a reform of religious practice begun but not completed in the hearts of all who profess belief is no reform at all. According to the Scriptures the reason for the fall of Jerusalem is that the reform did not take hold. And by "reform" is meant conversion or "change of heart."

The struggle to renew today's Church begun by the Fathers of Vatican II could fail as soon. Josiah is forgotten. If new members of the Church forget their call to continual self-renewal from within, so, too, may the renewal of the whole Church go without incident. Taken together, all of the external criticism of the Church today cannot effect so much as can the parish family through gentle persistence in practicing the holy faith they are continually learning to appreciate, understand, and live.

Advent

By some miracle you may be able to touch all the bases outlined above by the First Sunday of Advent so that Isaiah and Micah along with John the Baptist occupy center stage during the season of expectation. Perhaps the only effective way to fight the commercialism of Christmas is by highlighting the growth of messianism that occurs with the prophets just before and during the Babylonian exile. The hope for an anointed king of the house of David who would restore Israel to its former greatness and to a faithful relationship with Yahweh is the hope to be fulfilled. The season of plenty and prosperity, the return to home, and the restoration of families and kingdom show the tangible way that Israel came to expect that the Lord would produce for them. The developments in first, second, and third Isaiah and the other prophets in describing this temporal yet faithful messiah, along with the Catholic Church's use of these texts in the Prayer of Christians and in readings at the Eucharist, must be laid bare to our catechumens.

Also necessary for Advent and for this time in Israel's consciousness is the exposition of the growing feeling that Yahweh is God for everyone and that His saving power cannot be limited to national boundaries. The idea that He could and would use Israel as a light to all nations, to show them His glory and bring all to the truth does indeed mark a growth in faith. This idea is seized upon when the early Church runs into trouble with its own and accounts for Paul's success in convincing the Council of Jerusalem that Gentiles could be incorporated into the family of believers. For the prophets had foretold that Jesus had broken down every limitation and border to God's generosity.

Can you begin to understand the need for at least a two-year catechumenate? We have pushed to the limit to include the key elements in our family history, and yet the Psalms and the Wisdom literature have yet to be touched. In our time frame it is Christmas. The First Sunday of Lent is six to ten weeks away, and the catechesis has just begun!

There is no question but that the Psalms are their

own school of prayer and should be studied if we are ever to restore the Prayer of Christians to the Christians. The peculiar but engaging literature known as Wisdom literature is a sign of the influence of other cultures on Israel's conception of its faith. Important in itself the Wisdom literature is made even more important by its frequent use in our liturgy in symbolic and adapted ways. Though it can be confusing and misleading if not adequately treated, it can deepen the catechumen's understanding of the faith process.

All Scripture is a two-edged sword. It is important for understanding the vitality of the faith of our ancestors. It can as well be a prod and mirror for catechumens to deepen their own faith and become involved in the salvation story of which God is Author. Apropos is the story of the hopelessly crippled Black lady who somehow struggled to church on a nasty Easter Sunday. Asked by her priest why she had made the extraordinary effort when Communion could have been brought to her, she responded, "I come to hear that Easter story. I got to hear that story because Jesus did it for me."

This is *our* story. God did it for *us*. Not to tell it is to omit what God has done for those He loves. We are the *loved!*

Israel in the Time of Jesus

Following our development of the Scriptures' approach, we have next to do as good a job as possible describing Israel in the time of Jesus. Even the latest catechisms for adults seem to peak before they arrive at making His times and His personality real. Perhaps it is impossible to write it. I shrink from outlining what we have done lest I give the wrong impression. Again, we should keep in mind that the story of Jesus was preached, that is, told to individuals and groups. In preaching, the animation, the gestures, the personal conviction can mean as much as the words. Words from the mouth worked the magic of conversion in the early Church. That is why liturgists stress the importance of the Word proclaimed and the value of homilies that break open that proclamation.

One of the few gimmick exercises we have used with success is asking the group to describe their hometown at the time of their childhood: where they lived, where the rest of their relatives lived, whom they went to see when they were young, who ran the town, what the employment picture was, what were the housing and school settings of their early life, what the weather was like in summer and winter, how they traveled to places of interest, where they went for picnics or for vacation. All this is autobiographical and can be written and told or just told. In addition to awakening a little healthy nostalgia, it brings to the fore a considerable number of factors that require discussion if Jesus and His time are to assume human proportions.

The rugged terrain of Palestine, the herding and the fishing, the agrarian scene, the villages away from Jerusalem and Jerusalem's great Temple and market-place, the weather, the heat of the sun, the scarcity of potable water, the importance of wells, the relation-ship with neighboring tribes to the north—the whole setting and background are as important to under-standing Jesus' use of imagery and how He traveled as is L'Enfant's plan for the city of Washington for today's tourist to negotiate the circles, blocks, and quadrants of the city.

The political picture is important, too, for the

political background and the institutionalized religion are two sides of the same coin. The Roman occupation, the place of the imperial governors, and their political relationship with the Jewish high priests are factors that cannot be just skimmed if Jesus' teaching is to be appreciated. The conflict between Pharisees and Sadducees on the question of life after death, their relative roles in ruling the people, and the role of the scribes in an illiterate society are to be fathomed before Jesus' exchanges with these groups that find their way into the Gospel can ever be appreciated.

The Jesus we know as the Anointed, the Christ, lived in a time and a place that, to a colorful and important degree, formulated the way He taught, the miracles He chose to perform, and the kind of death He died. The catechumen, who comes from his or her own specific history and background, has the right to learn of Jesus in the same detail as his or her self-awareness. The picture of Jesus cannot simply be equated with the eternal existence of the Word, the Second Person of the Trinity. Jesus was born in Bethlehem, grew up in Nazareth, preached in Galilee and Judea, and died on a hill outside Jerusalem.

It takes time to present this background, and it takes creative imagination to present it in an (to coin a term) "unclassroomy" way. Maps, slides, and pictures help, but they are no substitute for the presentation which can be given by a student of the Scriptures who has made that world his or her own.

It does not take much research to determine that religious preachers enjoyed large audiences during Jesus' time. Our sophisticated society might term the religious preacher one of the few choices of entertainment then available in town and villages after a hard day's work. In fact, during the time Jesus was preaching, twenty or more preachers were claiming to be the long-awaited messiah. The picture of revival tents in various rural and small-town areas of our country comes to mind. The competition among so-called faith healers in this country today and the power they possess over segments of the public form a rough parallel to serve imagination. With all this background information, the way in which Jesus emerges from this pack both during His life and after the Resurrection becomes even more of a surprise.

Public Ministry of Jesus

If you were to describe the "whole of Catholic teaching" that the Rite of Christian Initiation requires catechumens to come to know, the public ministry of Jesus would certainly be a part of your outline. The proportion given to it in inquiry classes would compare, no doubt, with other important sections. In the catechumenate we are reminded that we are incorporating these new members into the mystery of Christ. The progress in conversion and in faith is to be celebrated in transition from stage to stage. The growth factor is the reason that the whole of Christian teaching is being presented. All of the Old Testament material and all that will be said about Jesus are not for comprehensive examinations but for faith, and faith, as we well know, is more than intellectual awareness or mastery. If for growth in faith any section of the catechumenate is more important than another, it is the section on the ministry of Jesus.

In any discussion of Jesus' teaching and activity, the catechist must "tune out" the old inquiry class process with its concerns for "making points" on the divinity of Jesus. If the Scripture and the tradition of the early Church are our guides, we begin with the human person who had the impact of a simple but forceful message. Jesus' divinity is an aspect of His personality that we should come to realize as did the early Church. The final step of faith is the recognition that Jesus the Lord is Lord of all. The cumulative effect of the preaching which became the Gospel leads to that faith.

The intermediate phases of growth are best developed in prayerful study of the Gospel. What is important to Jesus and to the early Church's memory of Jesus is patiently outlined either thematically or following the Synoptic plan. At various stages of this development the different discoveries of individuals in the catechumenate are shared and celebrated, both informally in prayer sessions with the group and formally in the Sunday Eucharists with the whole parish.

Using Mark as the basic Synoptic Gospel, we begin at his beginning: the preaching of John the Baptist. We save the infancy for last when it can be appreciated for what its narratives are in Matthew and Luke. The preached nature of the Gospel stories and the comparison of the Synoptics become clear from the study.

Important in this explanation of Jesus are the miracles and the teaching points that Jesus makes around those miracles. The presence of the kingdom of God, of the forces for healing and life in conflict with disease and death, is a much more important work than the wonder of the miracle itself. As much as possible the wonder of the crowds at His teaching should be emphasized rather than the picture of some who make Jesus into a freakish wonder-worker. No mention is ever made that Jesus worked miracles simply to impress. Miracles are worked for the faith-filled so that more persons may come to believe. The greatest "miracle" for Jesus, His greatest work, is to stimulate faith. This point can be illustrated by the numerous examples in the Synoptics. We suggest saving the Johannine material for the scrutinies later in the Rite, since they are miracle stories used in the period of enlightenment after the election, and their faith power builds on the earlier miracle stories in the Synoptics.

The miracles are intimately related to the teaching, and the Beatitudes and the Lord's Prayer are excellent beginning points for introducing Jesus' preaching of the kingdom. Matthew's Gospel, which is built around the kingdom themes, is an incredible joy to teach. Luke's ability to draw strong characters and to enrich his written work with human details can lead catechumens to reach out and embrace those characters as well as the Jesus of Luke's Gospel.

Key to making the distinction between the Christian and the world and key to the conversion process are Jesus' teaching and example of self-sacrifice and self-denial. What *The New American Bible* editors call the doctrine of the cross in Mark (with parallels in Matthew and Luke) has brought the self-denial theme to life for our catechumens. I refer to Mark 8:27-38, 9:30-32, and 10:32-45. Jesus' teaching about the cross and the stories that immediately follow highlight the true Christian spirit. They are texts that, taken together, turn back those nominal Christians who promise satisfaction, prosperity, and a cure-all in return for simply calling on the name of the Lord in faith. The Suffering Servant invites us to share the pain of disappointment, the frustrations with an unbelieving generation, and the rejections that came from His own in order to learn the power of His victory. Such an invitation!

The commitment and the quality of life that Jesus seeks is evident from the interview before the election with a twenty-eight-year-old woman who was married to a semipracticing Catholic. She recounted her reasons for initially joining the catechumenate in order to "have a religion and a religion that we could practice together."

But the catechumenate experience and the laying out of Jesus' invitation to take the cross and follow made her realize that the decision to go further in the process and to be incorporated into Jesus' death-resurrection would have some consequences that she could not avoid. One would be that her values would be different from those of practically all of her friends. Another difficulty was that she had to find a way to expose her Catholic husband to the conversion of life that is inherent in the Gospel message for those who are faithful. To be really committed would involve her in a program of prayer and activity that could cause family and friends to raise eyebrows and wonder. She is no fanatic—certainly no religious fanatic, nor is she interested in religious expressions or movements which have stirred controversy and reaction in Church circles. Her commitment to Christ, her possible election to celebrate those mysteries fully with the faith community would cause her to pay a price, a personal price; and she wanted the support of her priest-catechist and those who were involved with her in bringing that decision to fruition. That lady had experienced the teaching and the invitation. She expressed as well as any the choices and the content of the restored catechumenate.

The Passion Narratives

If possible, Lent and the Passion narratives make a nice pairing. The material on the events surrounding the suffering and death of Jesus takes us back to the Passover event and to all the material developed on that event in previous sessions. More importantly, it renews the feeling of the Jewish celebration family-style that what Yahweh had done He would continue to do for the Jew today. The basis for developing the presence of the Christ in the Eucharist and the panoply of Eucharist themes should be laid out now in this context and later in the Acts of the Apostles.

The story of Jesus' suffering and death has a force all its own, and the story needs no retelling here. All the force of the personal dynamics and conflicts should be explained, and our following of Jesus' life to this point without a lot of reference to the Christ or the divinity makes the human tragedy of these hours an experience that we humans can feel.

The Resurrection Accounts

The resurrection accounts should be treated in depth with the Acts of the Apostles in the final stage of the catechumenate: the mystagogic phase. But the witness of the early Church to the empty tomb and the confusion and bewilderment of the Twelve are integral to the meeting with Jesus, now the Christ, and to the formation of faith that precedes sacramental initiation. Here, as with the Gospel, the human dimensions of the reaction of the women and the Twelve are the factors that engage the catechumens to a full-blown faith. The element of surprise and shock at the empty tomb, heightened by the fear of that close-knit community that they could soon meet the fate of Jesus even as they huddled in the upper room, is part of the process of becoming convinced that Jesus is Lord and Master. The joy, the thrill of the eyewitnesses was communicated to the listeners who sought conversion and initiation.

The earliest preaching as found in Acts here becomes part of the immediate preparation for election and part of the urgency to use Lent as a true conversion and purification time for the catechumens. The debate at the Council of Jerusalem is important, for *these* catechumens are *those* Gentiles who are equal to the Jews because of their faith.

The persecutions of the first century are evidence of the literalness with which the early believers "took up the cross" and a quite credible apologetic of the veracity of their witness. In fact, the New Testament and the persecutions present a wealth of evidence that the perquisites attached to modern ministry were present in no discernible way to the first ministers of the early Church. Theirs was a difficult lot, and the presence of suffering among true believers today makes entrance into the Church an initiation into a community that is still ready to die for the Lord in spite of the ever-present signs of wealth observable in some quarters of the Church. The quiet but persistent persecution of Church leaders and members in certain countries of Central and South America and Africa gives credibility to the argument that we are the descendants of a Lord and a Church who were jailed, beaten, and tortured to death.

Development of Liturgy

In our catechesis the sacraments are treated as the ministry and work of the early Church. We trace the historical development of the sacraments of initiation (Baptism, Confirmation, Eucharist) through the study of the Acts of the Apostles. Orders of service in the Church as found in Acts need to be expanded historically to develop notions of priesthood more common to our contemporary Church than to the Acts of the Apostles. In all the talk of sacraments we are seeing their development in the context of the growth in self-understanding of the great sacrament, the Church.

Anointing of the Sick from the letter of James and the holiness of Marriage and its gradual development over the centuries show the ease with which the Church used the resources at its disposal to enrich the different situations of life. The sacrament of Reconciliation and its history from early penitential practice to today's face-to-face experience needs a good deal of time to explain fully.

The development of the sacraments beyond the breaking of the bread calls for an explanation of what for some is one of the more troubling concerns of the Acts of the Apostles and Paul's early letters. We are a Church that looks for the second coming of Christ, but we assume from the evidence of more than 1900 years that His coming will be in His own good time and in His fashion. The belief that Christ will come again is part of the earliest and most consistent content of faith. But the belief of the early Church was, for the first years of its existence, a belief that His coming would be very soon—in their lifetime. His failure to reappear after the Ascension caused some consternation and much reappraisal. It is a factor in the New Testament that must be treated and explained as evidence that, on this account, they were wrong and could admit it. So their early exhortations to remain as they were, single or married, until His coming were changed to a design for living and of celebrating sacraments "until He comes."

The Book of Revelation

The book of the Lord's coming, with its very strange imagery and apocalyptic overtones, is not to be avoided. We discuss the Book of Revelation not only because of its intrinsic worth as a message of hope and consolation to the seven churches but also because, in our day, so many fundamentalists use the book to scare persons into faith.

The Book of Revelation needs to be explained for what it is: an early second century call to hope in the Lord's coming in spite of the violent persecutions that unbelievers had inflicted on the fledgling Church. If we give catechumens the key to understanding this book, they will be able to disregard with confidence the ignorant and superstitious interpretations so many preachers give with such theatrical rhetoric. Even more than creating a clear understanding of it, we should bring the catechumen to see Revelation as the culmination of the family history.

Taken together, the Acts of the Apostles and the Book of Revelation are for the family of new covenant believers a legacy of how and why to keep up the struggle of faith in a fairly faithless age. Family activities and reasons for hope can best be outlined in the family of faith context which holds in the catechumenate.

Creeds and Heresies

The dire warnings in the New Testament writings against false teachers and preachers come to term in the development of early credal formulas. These expressions of faith were at first the direct result of worshipers giving voice to their common belief. The study of early liturgies and of some of the obvious liturgical expressions which found their way into the New Testament gives ample evidence that the praying community developed short statements of truth to put their faith into a common rendition.

The creation of such statements of belief is not over. In formal declarations and expository forms our conference of bishops repeatedly rephrases and re-expresses the faith of the Church on various issues. How many parishes advert to these statments or respond to them is quite another question. But a parish that is accustomed to formulating its faith in the risen Lord or its position on a moral choice confronting the local parish may well be in a position to respond effectively to the leadership of the Church when they speak.

Thus the practice of having the catechumens write their convictions from time to time in short statements is more than a spiritual exercise. It forces believers to fix their faith in words that can never express the total reality but can be compared for illumination to other statements in the history of the family of faith. Most importantly, the practice of developing credal formulas and moral positions can open the local church to similar statements from Church leadership and help the parish realize their role in serving the whole body of faith by expressing their convictions to their own ordinary. How can a bishop speak to the Church with truth and effectiveness if the local parishes are not speaking to one another and to him of their faith and insights?

The later creeds, such as the Nicene Creed and the Apostles' Creed, should be explained in their historical context. The reasons for the calling of the early ecumenical councils and the often violent nature of the political and religious quarrels that led to the development of doctrinal definition is a chapter in the family history that for many catechists and priests is readily avoidable. They simply choose to ignore it.

Yet Chalcedon and Nicaea, Florence and Trent are as important to contemporary faith as are Scripture studies or ethics. Failure to treat the history of heresies and their resolution renders the modern believer unable to understand adequately the tempest created by an Archbishop Lefebvre or the crossfire that occasionally occurs between more radical theologians and Church authority. Not to understand our history in this area of the development of faith is to leave believers disturbed and at a loss when confronted with contemporary disputes.

Ecumenical Collapse and Rebuilding

The Church, the body of Christ, is the key focus of the Rite of Christian Initiation, for it is into this body that the catechumen is to be initiated. The scandal of disunity, the pushing and pulling that ripped open the unity of believers, has to be appreciated by the catechumen for his or her understanding and for planting the seeds for reunification. The historical treatment of the 1054 split between East and West and the Protestant Reformation in the 16th century is absolutely vital to the appreciation of the unique position in which we find ourselves today. The threshold of unity with major Christian churches seems almost at hand. Is it too much to hope that by 2054 at least the Orthodox, the Anglican-Episcopalian, and the

Lutheran will with the Church of Rome comprise one body of faith?

The sharing of sacraments between Orthodox and Roman Catholic can be viewed as prelude to complete union. The work of the joint Anglican-Roman Catholic and Lutheran-Roman Catholic committees on Church unity has cleared the doctrinal path. Though the memories of crusades and heresy hunting, of the charges and countercharges, are receding, they are nonetheless aspects of a history that catechumens should know. Otherwise they will never understand why it has taken so long to begin to restore the unity of believers so integral to the New Testament record of early faith.

The issue of ordaining women to liturgical priesthood needs a balanced treatment because it is with us and will be with us. The true balance can be achieved under the ecumenical heading, for it is in this arena that the thorniest aspects of the debate surface. The position of the Episcopalians in the United States deserves a careful and patient study. Undoubtedly there are questions of rights, of cultural sexist practice, that render a conclusion obvious to this author but not so immediately obvious to the hierarchy. We used to criticize the Mormons for excluding Blacks from their highest Church offices while we claim to be following the Lord in excluding women from cultic priesthood.

But the question of achieving unity is a delicate balance of a fairly cosmopolitan nature. Both the backlash in the Episcopalian Church about ordaining women and the cultural and historical position of the Eastern Catholic Church on a married clergy, as well as some of the cultural conditioning in various countries that have a large membership in the Roman Catholic

Church, give one reason enough to pause before declaring anything so binding as to affect the worldwide Church.

The principle that must be felt in the catechumenate is one that has prevailed from the earliest days of the Church. We are one and catholic in our profession of faith and in our work for the kingdom. We are unlimited in our cultures and backgrounds, in our spiritualities and liturgies. A variety of expressions of worship is gradually becoming appreciated in our own country with the rapid rise of differing musical styles accompanying worship. Our catechumens can participate in children's liturgies, in a Mass with a Gospel choir, or in a Eucharist with a background in Gregorian chant. This variety, which serves a real purpose of ministering according to the ages and the tastes of all believers, has a parallel in the development of different liturgical expressions in different regions of the early Church.

If our catechumens are to be able to adapt to reasonable changes in the Church, the principle of meeting differing needs in different but agreed upon and approved ways must be taught. Pity the newly baptized who has been led to expect that the priest who baptized him or her will be in the same parish forever or that every parish or diocese does everything in exactly the same way!

It may well be that the Church of the future may have dioceses where an anticipated Sunday Mass on Saturday evening is not permitted. It is true today that a number of Catholic communities may not be permitted to celebrate the Eucharist but once a month because of the scarcity of priests or the remote location of the believing community. It may well be that our children's children will be permitted to celebrate Sunday Eucharist in an Episcopalian church in the United States united with Lutherans and Roman Catholics, and presided over by a duly ordained female priest. The challenge in it all is the challenge to work for what Jesus works, the kingdom of justice, of love, of peace.

Vatican I and Vatican II

Our catechumens will hear a lot about the Second Vatican Council. From resources available and from the Catholic and the secular media, they are constantly reminded that they are living in the wake of one of the more important pastoral events in the history of the Church.

Just as Jesus cannot be fully comprehended without the immediately prior history of Israel, so we cannot know ourselves and Vatican II without an awareness of the life of the Church tracing back to Vatican Council I. The differences and preoccupations of that time and place from our own are enormous. The differences parallel and are related to the growth of knowledge and technology that has occurred since Vatican I.

The comparison between the two worlds is illustrative not only of the changed atmosphere in the Church but also of the radically changed world in which we live. The First Vatican Council had to quit because of the threat of force. The Second Vatican Council had to debate politely whether or not it could afford to end its deliberations after ten years of meeting.

The impact of Vatican I was to redefine the Church's prerogatives in a time of severe attack. Vatican II described the position of a community of faith ministering the Gospel to a world in need and renewing itself to better proclaim the saving message and meet the requirements of a credible evangelization initiative.

Vatican II knew more about the needs of God's creation because of the power of an electric switch that, when turned on, plastered the plight of the poor and disenfranchised across a 21" diagonal screen of living color in the corner of a room. And the results of that Council, still being felt, are proof positive that this Church into which these catechumens are to be incorporated is a body that remains convinced that Jesus the Christ is as much the Anointed of Yahweh for this day as He was for the early Church. Times change. We need to know it. Yahweh is changeless. Our history tells us so.

Morality and Social Justice

The rights and wrongs of Christian living occupied fully a third of the available time in the convert class of old. The Ten Commandments of God and the Six Precepts of the Church were sixteen headings under which every conceivable topic of morality was discussed. Whatever problems anyone had with the approach of enunciating moral imperatives and explaining the same, one would be hard pressed to argue that they were unclear. When you talk with converts from the old instructional classes, you get a sense of appreciation for the simple, straightforward moral precepts that, for many, seemed to constitute the critical difference between Catholics and other Christians.

To argue for a developmental approach to morality, for the treatment of the way believers became more and more sophisticated in their common sense of right and wrong, may be futile. However, if you have

caught the flavor of the restored Rite of Christian
Initiation and the historical approach to the development of faith which is the process of theology and
Scripture studies today, you should realize that this
approach is laced with the moral teaching which we
have come to expect of Catholic life. Every phase of
our history as a chosen and saved people bears ample
witness to the constantly growing awareness that we
are called to a radically different life-style than that of
our unbelieving counterparts. So we do not come to a
final section in the catechumenate process and focus
on do's and don't's. Every historical phase adds a
refinement, a sense of heightened consciousness to
what has gone before.

It is clear to us that the historical treatment of the
development of morality can save us from falling into
the sins of our faith ancestors. The heavy insistence on
the social impact of sin in our own time recalls the
teaching of the prophets of the Old Testament. If the
Old Testament concern for justice, for the care of
aliens in the midst of Jewish people of old had been
an influential component of our treatment of slaves in
the New World, would we have been spared inflicting
second-class citizenship in the Church and in society
on the baptized slaves of the last century?

Knowing the history of moral development is to
recognize the really prophetic in our time as the ones
who espouse the rightness of a cause and are willing
to pay the price of rejection and even disbelief on the
part of religious persons as well as secular society. If
Jesus is bold enough to criticize the religious establishment of His own day as those who killed the
prophets, we need to share with our catechumens the
reasons that prophets, including Jesus, have been
killed. And this sharing is done in the same breath as

telling the story of our family.

Abraham is not our model of sexual morality but a model of faith in a God greater than all other gods. The Ten Commandments are not the last word on the moral law for growth in holiness. They are but the beginning of a body of national laws that were meant to insure the fidelity of a whole people to Yahweh and the right ordering of relationships among that people. The determination of the prophets that the care of widows, orphans, and the poor is a holy activity that united the people of God and insured both their moral and physical salvation is no less timely today. And the prophets' spirit cannot be captured in a simple recitation of precepts.

If the Black Church understands the prophetic call to holiness, it is because they have at times suffered more at the hands of allegedly Christian peoples than other parts of the Church. Martin Luther King preached the undiluted message of the prophets with the nonviolent imperative of Gandhi and the willingness to suffer for Christ. And many Catholics thought he was preaching a strange morality!

Knowing the history of our moral growth is knowing that we have come from polygamy to monogamy, from polytheism to monotheism, from waging war for Promised Lands to espousing an end to the arms race before we destroy ourselves. It is to feel the growth from the Decalogue to the Beatitudes, from a Moses who in faith could fight the Canaanites to a Jesus who could endure the Roman form of capital punishment. It is to appreciate that sexual ethics are an important aspect of moral life but not the exclusive concentration of morality. For sexual excess can divert and distress those whose calling is to make the kingdom happen.

The goal of the Rite of Christian Initiation is conversion, *metanoia,* the complete change that the earliest sermons in the Acts of the Apostles require before Baptism. All of the prayers and petitions for the catechumenate phase, as well as for the period of purification and enlightenment that follows, revolve around that required conversion. All of the history, all of the Scripture, all of the doctrinal development, all liturgical studies are for changing the way the believer approaches life. They provide the rationale—and a compelling one it is—for living the new life.

Bringing the Catechumenate to a Close

The area of parish Church life that requires review as the catechumenate comes to a close is the centrality of sacraments in the life of the Catholic Church. Few catechumens come quickly to see how Christ is present as the assembled community gathers to hear the Word or recall the death of the Lord until He comes. The Jewish notion of the presence of Yahweh in covenant renewal celebrations and in the Passover meal has prepared the potential convert for the experiencing of Christ in the Eucharist or the other sacraments. The history of the Protestant Reformation may well have brought home the tenacity of the Catholic Church in holding to a real presence of Christ in the seven explicit sacraments. But those special moments require a detailed treatment both in their institution and in their historical development. Each sacrament fits a need in the life of the Church, and each should be celebrated or at least witnessed by the catechumenate.

Third Stage:
Purification and Enlightenment

The Election

THIS next stage of the initiation process commences with the rite of election. Election? Even in a society that features elections as a staple of civic activity, the "rite of election" could have a strange ring to the Catholic ear. Cardinals elect popes. The Conference of Bishops elect a president. Most parishes elect their council. But why speak of an election for those seeking membership in the Church?

The words of the Rite of Christian Initiation are clear:

> At the beginning of Lent, which is the time of proximate preparation for sacramental preparation, the election or enrollment of names is celebrated. In this rite the Church hears the testimony of the godparents and catechists. After the catechumens reaffirm their intention, then the Church passes judgment on their state of preparation and states whether they may go on to the Easter sacraments (*RCIA*, 133).

The Church passes judgment. The decision is whether or not to incorporate fully these catechumen members into the body of the chosen by allowing them to celebrate the Easter sacraments (Baptism, Confirmation, Eucharist) with the community of faith. It is clearly the responsibility of the community of faith, the parish, which has formed and informed these catechumens to decide on their level of preparation and readiness to "take the plunge" into the death-resurrection of Christ.

The initiation Rite calls the "election" a matter of great concern for the catechumens and a matter to be weighed carefully by the whole parish. The decision to enroll a particular catechumen among the elect is a choice to be made by the whole Church, and the Rite spells out all who are involved: bishop, presbyters, deacons, catechists, godparents, and the whole community. Underlining the phrase *the whole community* will not of itself add the proper emphasis. It means not only going from the "Father Smith Instructs Jackson" approach to an approach as we have outlined in the preceding chapter on the catechumenate. It is also a matter of deciding whether or not Jackson should be baptized by a judgment involving the bishop and the whole community.

We come to the heart of the revised Rite, to the reason those who have studied it can rightly say that this ritual has the power to revolutionize our Catholic approach to the definition of a parish. If the whole community has the responsibility to elect, then the whole community has the responsibility to form new members. One of the requirements of belonging to a chosen people is to minister to prospective members in such a direct fashion that you can, in turn, choose others to be numbered among the chosen. The picture is of an evangelizing community that has built up an experience of adding new members to itself repeatedly and of each member having some experience of godparenting, that is, of sharing their faith and prayer life with a person coming to belief.

In a parish where an increasing number of members have shouldered this adult faith responsibility, it takes little imagination to see this year's godparents being listened to intently as they give their testimony on behalf of their catechumen. Having had the experience of traveling with another adult who has been initiated, you know what to listen for in the testimony of these godparents and how to make judgments when negative observations are raised. You, as a member of this parish, have had repeated opportunities to make the acquaintance of the catechumens after Sunday Eucharist or in the performance of the Christian service ministry that has involved the catechumen. Even if you have not had the chance to get to know this catechumen intimately, you are expected to become involved in an all-important decision. You become involved in approving the godparents and in weighing their reports as well as the reports of the catechists and the presbyters.

In all honesty, we at Saints Paul and Augustine parish have not yet reached this lofty pinnacle of parish involvement. But we are headed in that direction because it is constitutive not of the Rite but of what a parish should be capable of performing. We are at the stage (described in *RCIA*, 137, 138) wherein deliberation (in fact several deliberations) are held by catechist, priest, coordinator, godparents, and catechumens themselves on the suitability of the candidates. We hold these deliberations in the weeks just prior to the First Sunday of Lent. We are about to require the elected representatives of the parish council to take part in this decision or election.

The Rite makes it clear that the most important ministry in this phase of initiation is that exercised on behalf of the parish and the catechumen by the godparent. What we have stated before about godparent and sponsor deserves repeating here. We have decided that the choice of godparents by the catechumens with the consent of the priests is important. When the choice of the catechumen is for a godparent who is part of our parish and who is able to participate with the total process of initiation, the godparent and sponsor are one and the same.

When the catechumen has a faith relationship with a person he or she desires as a godparent but that person cannot, for whatever reason, participate directly in the formative process, then we generally accept the catechumen's choice of *godparent*. However, we do insist on a parishioner becoming *sponsor* for the catechumen and participating in the formative process to the same degree called for by the godparents in the Rite. We have found that the sponsor usually ends up being more influential and closer to the catechumen than the catechumen's choice of godparent.

An example may be illustrative. One of our catechumens (let us call her Betty) worked with a Catholic friend who apparently had a sincere interest in Betty's becoming a Catholic. The only place they met was at work, since the Catholic friend lived twenty miles away from Betty and was not a social friend. The Catholic took an almost maternal interest in Betty's reports of her catechumenate experiences but was a source of real distraction to Betty. Her questions left Betty so confused that one evening she came in tears to the group. She felt that she would never understand the Legion of Decency, the idea of novenas, or the League of the Sacred Heart. She wondered when she would have to make the pledge to avoid condemned movies and whether movies rated "R" were all to be boycotted.

The need for a sponsor from the Catholic membership of our parish was never clearer. Betty needed someone who knew where she was in formation and where the program was going. So Betty and I discussed the various Catholics involved in the program, and she picked one in whom she had confidence and with whom she developed a comforting and friendly relationship in short order. When the day of her election and the day of her initiation were celebrated, Betty had her godparent-friend on one side and the sponsor from the parish on the other.

What cannot be assumed is that every catechumen is ready to be elected to participation in the Easter sacraments. In spite of every effort to make the process of initiation a true conversion of life, a real journey in faith, a deep process that involves more than just intellectual understanding, it is quite possible that a number of catechumens can come to the time of election as if it were the time of exams.

The temptation to ride on the catechumenate as if on a merry-go-round is difficult to avoid for some types of persons. The prospective convert who is married to a Catholic and wants to become Catholic to present a unified approach on religion to the children needs help at this part of the process to insure that the most personal decision is coming from within, not from without. The adolescent who is in Catholic high school must be aware of the possibility of peer pressure. In short, every catechumen must be given breathing room at this point to stand for election by the community or to wait a while. Even those catechumens most faithful in attendance are not always those ready to celebrate the saving activity of Christ.

A priest who has not been directly involved in the process may be just the person to give the catechumen a sense of not disappointing others by opting out, at least for a while. Perhaps another catechist or the sponsor can give this breathing room to the candidate. Some need only a few weeks to come to a free decision. Some need more time. If the catechumenate process recycles itself within the parish, it reduces the fear of having to wait a long time.

At Saints Paul and Augustine we are currently structured in such a way that we normally celebrate election on the First Sunday of Lent with initiation at the Easter Vigil. We can and have adopted a fallback position in the one-year cycle to observing election at Easter and initiation at Pentecost, the only other traditional point of entry in the liturgical year. The catechumen who needs a little time may seize upon the availability of such a possibility.

As the catechumenate program lengthens, the necessity for periodic personal conversations with the catechumen will increase. The danger is that catechist and priest may have a very positive mind-set about the desire of "their" catechumens, and the participants may need an independent believer to confide in or to jolt them out of a merely intellectual pursuit. The intervention of priest or catechist who is not directly involved, paralleling the extraordinary confessor for religious communities, may well provide an antidote to an enthusiasm which may veil true intentions. In any event, the catechumen needs to come to a choice independently of the local parish.

These decisions on the part of parish and catechumen are important for more than initiation six weeks hence. Once the decisions are made, the parish and the elect are bound together in a union for the Lenten observance, whose goal can be simply stated: conversion. It is almost stated that the parish needs the elect in order to prepare properly for the renewal of their own baptisms at the Easter Vigil. The elect are to look to the faithful for an example. In this season, the parish is to show the elect the deepest meaning of total conversion. The presence of the elect in the daily

128

gatherings of the parish is stimulus enough to longtime Catholics to rediscover the meaning of their own
initial coming to faith. During Lent Eucharistic liturgies
and prayer services must be structured so as to afford
Catholics and elect the opportunity to share their
insights and feelings.

The period is called by two names: purification and
enlightenment. These terms refer to the oldest traditions in the Church and in the history of the catechumenate. As aware as the Church is for both in its
members, it is quite simply wrong to see purification
and enlightenment for the elect alone. The whole
Church is engaged in purification from the Ash
Wednesday call to repent and fast to the Holy Week
celebration of reconciliation. This is not a period for
repeated celebrations of the sacrament of Reconciliation for the Catholic. Lent with the elect is a six-week
preparation for reconciliation, a holy time of examin-
ing personal and parish activities and modes of thinking to bring about the closest possible relationship
with Christ and His way.

And as the Eastern Church sees the process of
coming to faith as a coming into the true light of the
risen Christ, so, too, is it for those already baptized.
The light into which we have come can be rendered
even brighter when we are involved in bringing others
into Christ. The old axiom that the teacher learns as
much as, if not more than, the student is apropos of
the Lenten period of enlightenment. In the lively
exchange between a penitent parish and the elect, the
youngest in faith may bring more light to the total
parish than those who have been through Lent num-
berless times. They certainly bring reason enough for
enthusiasm for making Lent a period of purification
and enlightenment.

Enrollment Liturgy

THE most striking feature of the liturgy of election is the insistence on testimony from all parties involved. No other Roman liturgical experiences are designed like a church meeting. This liturgy, held on the First Sunday of Lent, is dialogue pure and simple: a public proclamation of the local church in their own faith and in the activities of these catechumens. There is no question that the authors of this service want those who plan it to adapt the Rite to the circumstances of the local parish—to change the words and introduce symbolic activity that has meaning for these candidates and this parish.

The Rite is constructed around the following dialogue and activity: presentation of candidates by the representative; calling by name of candidates; an opportunity for testimony by godparents, local congregation, and catechumens themselves. Enrollment of the names in the book of the elect follows directly. The Rite closes with a final exhortation to the elect and their godparents and a prayer for the elect in the form of the General Intercessions. After the elect are excused or in their presence (according to local custom), the Eucharist is celebrated.

Next to the dialogue the element that fascinates us most is the direction that the presiding person in this assembly is the bishop or his delegate. The bishop stands for the whole Church, for all believers in this diocese, and, in his membership in the college of bishops, for all believers in the Catholic world. His presence, therefore, is one of the whole Church in the faith activity of this parish. While the whole parish has been the prime framework for this catechumenate journey, the presence of the bishop at the election clearly states that membership in this parish is membership in the whole community of believers. The Rite of Christian Initiation thus provides for the pedagogically sound principle of moving from particular to general—from the individuals we know to that larger assembly of the whole Church, who, we can now know, share the same faith and work as we.

The activity of the bishop in this Rite brings to the fore the earliest functions of the bishop. It is not the bishop who elects these catechumens to Easter initiation. The bishop provides the forum for the local parish to state their intention to initiate these catechumens and the reasons that have led them to decide to do so. The bishop does not even have to write their names in the book of the elect. His is a witness of the whole Church to this activity.

More than a witness, the bishop ratifies and supports the decision of the local parish. His presence is encouragement to the local parish that their efforts at spreading the Gospel and forming new members in the Gospel way are of the essence of Church membership. In his homily before the Rite, the bishop explains the significance of election and by admitting the elect makes the decision of the parish the decision of the whole Church. His blessing on this process is both sanction and push to the entire parish to continue as they have begun in their Gospel ministry.

The bishop as ratifier and supporter is a definition that only half facetiously could be expanded to say he is the cheering section of the Church for this parish. The image of the bishop implementing this Rite in the parishes of his dioceses and then coming to the elections in various parishes to assess the impact of the restored Rite is here envisioned. His presence at meetings of catechumens prior to the rite of election is desirable. It is the bishop who has the responsibility of setting the period of time and directing the discipline of the catechumenate (*RCIA*, 20).

The Rite hopes that the bishop will be able to be present with the elect at the celebration of initiation at the Easter Vigil. In a sense, the whole process of initiation is his doing. He implements and sets the time for the program, appoints worthy catechists, and ratifies the election of the local parish. Certainly this assignment will begin to take more and more of the bishop's time, but it will make more obvious the chief pastoral function the bishop exercises in his diocese.

Practical Considerations

As more and more parishes implement the restored Rite, the presence of the bishop on the First Sunday of Lent in all these parishes is likely to prove impossible. He can delegate this function to an auxiliary or to vicars, but the feeling that the whole Church is present, even though the bishop himself is not, should be maintained. A letter delegating an auxiliary or a vicar should be read, and the ordinary should certainly meet those elected during the Lenten period. As the Church in America faces the question of children's Confirmation and attempts to restore the primitive order of the sacraments of initiation, we should be mindful that the restored Rite makes more demands on the bishop's time than does the celebration of adolescent Confirmation. Time must be given the chief pastor to take a personal, pastoral initiative in both implementation and operation of this process.

If the demands of evangelization and initiation are too great on ordinaries of larger dioceses and archdioceses, reform in the size of such jurisdictions seems indicated. Otherwise, the implementation of the process of initiation will miss a key element; namely, the confidence that the local parish is doing the work of the whole Church because the whole Church is present at key points in the process in the person of the bishop.

The pastor needs to add two new items to records and registers kept in the office safe. Next to the Baptism, Confirmation, First Communion, Marriage, and Death registers are now added a Register of

Catechumens and the Book of the Elect. The Book of
the Elect should be one that a pastor is not embar-
rassed to use in liturgical rite and place on the altar or
in the lap of the ordinary. We use a large, leather-
bound scrapbook with the title *The Book of the Elect*
lettered handsomely on the cover.

The sponsor and/or godparent exercise their first
public ministry at the rite of election. Again, these
ministers are chosen with the active involvement and
consent of the priest and, as far as possible, with the
consent of the entire community (*RCIA,* 136). They are
called by name before the bishop and testify to the
whole assembly on the suitability of their catechumens. They may even write their names in the Book of
the Elect as godparents.

More importantly, the restored Rite makes the
godparent/sponsor the permanent friend and, if the
words were not so negative in another context,
accomplice or fellow traveler of the catechumen in the
journey to initiation *and beyond.* It is the sponsor,
already close to the candidate because of "example,
character, and friendship," who walks the candidate
through election, the Lenten period of purification
and enlightenment, and the period of postbaptismal
catechesis (*mystagogia*)(*RCIA,* 43). It is the godparent
who is constantly at hand even after the process is
complete to assist with advice, shared prayer, and
Christian friendship. For the process is never really
complete. The process of Christian initiation becomes
in the next Lent the process of reinitiation, of prayerful preparation through fasting and hearing the Word
for experiencing again the newness of life in Christ.

Think of the implications for the local parish when
the number of parishioners who exercise the ministry
of godparent-sponsor grows. Just suppose that in a

parish of a thousand families you have a hundred who have exercised or are exercising this ministry. The ministry is full-time and, as we have said, demands a formation period. But the results are that the local parish increasingly becomes solicitous of the strength and condition of every member. As more and more baptized Catholics exercise this ministry, as more and more find their way to parish councils and to leadership in parish organizations, the concern of the whole parish will be directed to the quality of faith of the members, not in any meddling fashion but in developing the support systems for the living out of the Christian way. Then the host of wonderful pastoral programs that have been developed in the Church in America will be given a new focus. Parish programs for marrieds and singles, for teens and seniors, for charismatics and cursillistas, for ministers of social justice and those interested in adult religious education will be seen for what they are and given an integrating principle. This parish exists actively to support the faith life of its members and continually to add new members who are attracted to Christ because of the way the community acts that meets in His name.

Idealistic? It is only as much so as the Christian community described in the Acts of the Apostles. Take it slowly, in portions that you can comfortably bite into. Then the ministry of godparent-sponsor approved by the whole parish can and will become the ministry that has more day-to-day influence on the quality of parish life than the other restored ministries in proclamation, song, Eucharist, and even catechist. This is a ministry for every adult Christian, a ministry that separates the committed, but struggling, from the routine Catholic.

Celebrating Election

THE elect themselves should readily celebrate their election. Perhaps normally reticent in public, they would hesitate to occupy center stage. But repeated introductions to the local community in Sunday Eucharists and other celebrations in which they have been prayed for serve to create a comfortable feeling in the elect. If they are unwilling to say much in public, protesting shyness, they can have godparents-sponsors speak about their intentions. A favorite ploy to involve the reluctant is to take some incident from the catechumenate which illustrates the faith of the particular catechumen and share it with the assembled community at the election or during one of the scrutinies.

During Lent the elect exercise an implicit ministry all their own. From the suggested prayers in the rite of election, it is clear that the elect are the sign to the whole parish of what Lent is to be about. This group is chosen by the chosen not only to be initiated but also to give them their orientation to six weeks of penance and reflection. We have the presence of the elect, the questions put to them, and the testimony they offer about their conversion and their reasons for choosing to live the Christian life. Experience with the Rite has led us to the conclusion that Lent without elect is half Lent. Lent with elect is a parish program in itself, and it should not be compromised by any national or diocesan programs that distract the parish focus from initiation and reinitiation. We as a parish family are preparing our hearts and minds for a fresh reinitiation into the saving death-resurrection by leading the elect to their initiation. Their experience of the deep liberation from sin that Christ accomplishes in us is our experience all over again at new levels.

Finally, we should not underestimate the power of the Rite to engage those apparently least interested, namely the pew-warmers occupying the last rows in the church. Seeing the importance attached to the celebration of election with the various parish ministers associated with the bishop, many are prompted to raise questions with the priest or others involved in the presentation of the elect. A gentle nudge for those already Catholic in the direction of the catechumenate may well be indicated.

In our parish a number of non-Catholics find their way to the liturgies of Lent, Ash Wednesday, and Holy Week. The presence and involvement of the elect become a recognizable group with whom they can identify. We have instances—repeated instances—of acquaintances, family members, and total strangers being so moved by the celebration of election or of the Easter Vigil rite of initiation that they request entry into the catechumenate then and there. Nothing prohibits them from joining the weekly sessions to get a feel for the process. Once in, they usually stay into the next cycle.

On the other hand, there is nothing to keep the newly initiated from spending one year in the catechumenate even after the postbaptismal catechesis. We had a young lady go through the program of her own initiation and then remain for the next year with her mother. We thought she was there to give her mother transportation. She made it clear, however, that she considered the sessions important for herself personally because "I missed so much the first time around."

The enrollment liturgy complete with all the ministers, including the bishop, is an impressive act of faith. If the bishop is unable to be with the parish at the actual initiation, the liturgy of enrollment may seem anticlimactic to the Vigil and its initiatory rites. Not so! All the moments of celebration of initiation have their own significance and their unique beauty.

We who have been brought up on the *ex opere operato* theory of sacraments might indeed give too much emphasis to one or another aspect of the celebration. We might find ourselves overly preoccupied, for instance, with the actual words that effect the Christ action. Years of waiting for *Hoc est enim corpus meum*, of listening for "I baptize you" and attaching the total significance of the sacramental action to a few words could lead us to deprecate the value of all that goes before and follows the moment of pronouncing certain words. Who among us would argue that the recitation of marriage vows is *the* point in the substance of a loving relationship? Hopefully, the significance of the relationship was realized long before the recital of vows. It will deepen and grow in the way of life to follow.

There is a sense in which every sacrament celebrates an event that has already taken place. It is surrounded by other events. We repent our sins and decide to celebrate reconciliation and Penance. We are called to Orders as priest or deacon and freely decide in response to the bishop's call to celebrate that call to an ordered way of life in the liturgy of a sacrament. The Eucharist of the Last Supper is a remembering and re-presentation of a once-for-all event: the death/resurrection of the Lord (as is every sacrament). We celebrate what has taken place and in mystery is remembered and re-lived sacramentally. What took place in the life of the Redeemer of mankind passes over into the sacraments.

So with Christian initiation. The decision to be baptized and to baptize is certainly to be regarded as most important, the necessary prelude and reason for the actual Baptism itself. So true is this that the avowed catechumen is regarded as having embraced the life of faith and is entitled to marriage in the Church or to Christian burial even before Baptism. The process of coming gradually to appreciate the Christ is marked by repeated celebrations both within the catechumenate and during the period of illumination. The Rite, as we shall soon see, carefully draws us from any fixation on one moment in the process over other moments. We are instructed that the challenge of Christian living is ongoing and not to be reduced to the pouring of water but to be enhanced by a panoply of signs that express the fullness of Christian life.

The Presentations

THE Rite calls for the presentation of the Creed after the first scrutiny and of the Lord's Prayer after the third scrutiny in accord with the oldest practice (*RCIA*, 53). These so-called "presentations" are moments of precious sharing. They are a "tradition," a handing over of Christian treasures as gifts to the elect. With them the faith community shares their cherished beliefs and most inspired prayer—the Lord's own prayer. Following the counsel of the Rite, we have made the presentations in the time of the catechumenate in a less formal manner. But the presentations during the period of purification and enlightenment have a lot more than antiquity to recommend it. The Creed suggested as the one that expresses the community's faith shared with the elect is the Apostles' Creed. In its simplicity and directness it has a lot to offer to both elect and baptized. Are we losing our memory of this prayer? It might become an "endangered species"! We say the Nicene Creed so much at Mass that many Catholics get confused when called to lead or pray the Apostles' Creed. And this occurs even with those who pray the rosary daily! The presentation of the Creed may well take us back to the simplicity of the Apostles' Creed in our Eucharistic celebrations.

The presentation of the Lord's Prayer evokes a favorite saying of a holy Jesuit patron of the poor in Washington, Father Horace McKenna, that the Our Father is the union card of all Christians, immediately recognizably throughout the world regardless of language.

Both the statement of faith and the Lord's Prayer are so central to the life of the Church that they should be presented in an assembly of the entire faithful. Whether occurring during this period of illumination or earlier in the catechumenate, the occasion calls for a homily on the meaning of the respective prayers. Recited by elect and parish alike, they forge even more deeply the bonds that unite the new believer with the community.

Scrutinies of the Elect

THE celebration of the scrutinies is held on the Third, Fourth, and Fifth Sundays of Lent because the scrutinies celebrate the transforming power of Christ as captured in the readings for those Sundays. The readings for these three Sundays are always taken from the Year A Cycle when the elect are present. Parenthetically, one of the reasons for a three-year process of Christian initiation is undoubtedly having the experience of hearing the full Lectionary proclaimed in assembly.

The Gospel readings on these three Sundays in cycle A are from John's Gospel, the Gospel that presents the great signs Jesus worked to lead the people to faith. John's genius is in stylistically creating an elaborate dialogue on two levels between Jesus and the person seeking faith. The exchange between the two begins with the simple and apparent, and John develops the conversation in such a way that Jesus leads the person from what is apparent to the deeper faith-level. In fact, the Gospel according to John is a handbook of faith, composed late in the first century to show the Church how to understand the signs Jesus worked and how to use those signs to bring more and more people to faith.

I will leave the exegesis of these readings to the commentaries, with a plug for the most recent work of Father Raymond Brown, S.S., on John's Gospel.[5] Let me make the more obvious connections between the readings and the elect who are on the verge of full incorporation.

First off, the scrutinies are not a series of questions, as the term might imply. Rather they are the prayerful extension of the Scripture readings into the lives of the elect. A liturgy of the Word: readings, homily, prayer for the elect, and prayer of exorcism are designed as the final phrase of the conversion experience for the elect and for the whole parish preparing for the Easter event.

Much of the power of the scrutinies can be lost when the deacon or the priest reads the short form of the appointed Gospels. If anything, these Gospels should be proclaimed in their fullness, and consideration should be given to their most effective presentation, say, with various parts taken by different readers in imitation of the three-part presentation of the Passion. What is vital is to achieve the proclamation of the full story.

Living Water. Perhaps you should open your handy pocket Lectionary to the Third Sunday of Lent in the Year A Cycle. Here you can begin to see the relationship between the readings and the elect. I would like to reflect for a minute to offer some suggestions for a homily (depending on the pace of the homilist) on these readings as if we were celebrating the first scrutiny. These are suggestions, remember—not a model homily (is there such a thing?).

> The recurring symbol in the first and third readings today (tonight) is water, the symbol of initiation for the elect. The first reading (Exodus 17:3-7) has more than preliminary interest. It is quite obviously a *thirst* story. It is also a *freedom-from-slavery* story, a story that recounts the Israelites' deep dissatisfaction with being free if freedom means death

for them, their children, and their livestock. In our parish, founded with the help of President Abraham Lincoln, we are able to understand more readily than most people, the price of freedom from slavery than could be in the case in less historic parishes. Freedom and salvation have a price: Yahweh will take care of the basics like water for the nation that is willing to be responsible and free.

It is rare that anyone would lay down his life for a just person, though it is barely possible that for a good person someone may have the courage to die. It is precisely in this that God proves His love for us: that while we were still sinners (unjust, not good), Christ died for us (Romans 5:7-8).

The elect have already been justified by their faith. They are already at peace with God because of their beginning membership in the community of the saved. There is no disappointment. The love of God is already poured out in our hearts.

Now we turn to the Gospel of the Samaritan woman at the well (John 4:1-42):

What a piece of good news! Those voted least likely to succeed in the prevailing opinion of Jerusalem were the Samaritans, the heretics of the Old Testament. To find a Samaritan in the spotlight with Jesus is surprising enough. But to have a woman coming to salvation and ministering salvation to her townsfolk by introducing them to Jesus is a culture shock in Jesus' time that the most enthusiastic feminist supporter cannot describe. In a city and a congregation where women are more than a simple majority, the presence of this woman is a living, compatible invitation to faith in the Anointed. Even more to the point for some of the elect, and some of those Catholics participating, is the woman's marital status. Five husbands!

Though I might not make this point in a homily, it is a point that needs making. The person who comes to you seeking faith and salvation may come from a complicated series of relationships including prior marriage.

Our first responsibility is to show them the Christ. If faith happens, if the person can pay the price of being a true Christian and demonstrates that he or she can do so by fidelity to the process of Christian initiation, may we not assume that the Lord will make the *past* something that has *passed?*

Our responsibility is aptly summarized here: you may think you are married, but you are not. It is a simple fact. It is not a reason to stop the faith dialogue but a compelling reason to continue. The Church in tribunals and leadership has enough consistency to maintain Christ's teaching on the indissolubility of true marriage, while at the same time reconciling new believers to the Church and to a marriage that meets the definition of Christian marriage.

Let us get back to the homily.

The "living water" that Jesus speaks of and the "flowing water" of the woman are a baptismal dialogue that recalls both Old Testament history and New Testament fulfillment. The fountain that leaps up to provide

eternal life should be in front of the congregation so that the homilist can point to it. It
should be empty on the Third Sunday of
Lent; so should the holy water fonts. But the
visibility of the empty font or pool is the
occasion for the most effective homily on
what Jesus will provide the elect in Baptism.
The empty font creates anticipation of the
Easter Vigil when the blessing of the font will
be highlighted.

Again, parenthetically, has your parish built
a reconciliation room in keeping with the
revision of the sacrament of Penance? Most
parishes have, sometimes at too great a cost.
The relative speed with which we created the
conditions for face-to-face celebration of Reconciliation while preserving the option for
anonymity can only be admired.

The order went forth as to when the new
rite of Penance must be implemented, and
the bottom line gave the firm date when it
had to be implemented. The published norm
for Baptism by immersion of the body ante-
dates the revision of the sacrament of Penance. Sadly, there is no bottom line on when
immersion of the body in water, living water,
is to be implemented.

So we are treated to the spectacle of a table
with a bowl and a shell appearing and disap-
pearing in the sanctuary for infant baptisms at
Sunday Mass. Taking adult baptism as the
norm and providing for Baptism by immersion will, no doubt, take the creative genius
of our ministers of church architecture. But
the Church everywhere is replete with mod-

els, and the implementation of this decreed norm should proceed lest Jacob's well and living water that provides eternal life remain figments of imagination in the consciousness of most believers.

The homily shifts from water to food, from eternal life to "Doing the will of him who sent me and bringing his work to completion is my [Jesus'] food" (John 4:34). What better description is there of the Eucharist, the initiation into doing the work of Yahweh!

You elect will be plunged into the living waters of the risen Christ and will feed on His body, the food of those who are busy bringing Yahweh's work to completion. (You do not even hear this part of the Gospel or what follows if you read the short form.)

There is another important element for the elect and the parish before the concluding recognition that this Jesus "is the Savior of the world" (John 4:42). The water and the food and the work lead naturally to something for all to see: "The fields are shining for harvest!" (John 4:35). Our preoccupation with evangelization has no better expression. John was well aware by the end of the first century that some sow and some reap. In the presence of our own reality we are able to make that statement ours. The elect are our harvest, and the sowing of the seed of faith has normally been the work of others. Even as we celebrate this harvest, we realize that we are sowing what others may reap. Just as others may have prompted these elect to faith, we are prompting others to faith whom we may never know.

The prayer that follows is the prayer of the congregation for the elect. The godparent's sign of touching his or her catechumen is one of the community's signs of support for the completion of the conversion process in the lives of the elect.

The prayer of exorcism mentions the Samaritan woman and the thirst of the elect for the living waters of Baptism. The petition is one for complete change of orientation in their lives to life in the Spirit, the way to salvation. The imposition of hands by the priest is another sign of the community's sharing with the elect the power of the risen Christ which they have received.

Fire and Light. The second scrutiny picks up another element of the Easter Vigil service of initiation: fire and light. The story of the man born blind (John 9:1-41) has the same Johannine dynamic that begins with the obvious and moves to faith. Christ is the light. A second element of anointing, present in the first scrutiny, surfaces here. Thereby both first and third readings allude to the chrism of Confirmation.

The first reading for the Fourth Sunday of Lent (1 Samuel 16:1-13) is the Lord's election and anointing of the least likely of Jesse's sons, the handsome young David. Samuel, a creature of his own culture, thought Jesse's heir Eliab would become the Lord's anointed. Working the two levels of appearances and faith, the Lord makes it clear that He sees the inner workings of the heart as more important. The hearts of the elect and the parish are here being transformed in this Lenten journey in faith, and, as always, those considered least likely to possess the Lord are those whom He elects to do the greatest works. David is anointed, "and from that day on, the spirit of the Lord rushed upon David" (1 Samuel 16:13).

The implications for the faithful are clear: we are a kingly race, an openhearted people whom the Lord elects to do His work.

There was a time when we were in darkness, but now we are light in the Lord (to paraphrase the reading from Ephesians). Already the elect are in the light. Faith has overcome the dark deeds of night. The shameful deeds are behind us. Here it would be visually helpful to have the large, unlit, undecorated paschal candle in a place where the congregation can see it and the homilist refer to it.

The Gospel (John 9:1-43) is more than the story of coming from blindness to sight, but that theme is the burden of the Good News for this congregation and the elect. It is almost a challenge to the blindness of those who think themselves religious, a timely reminder to the total parish that the *elect* among them may be closer to true conversion than those who have been at the practice of religion for years.

The Gospel attacks those allegedly religious persons who consider their position to be deserving of respect simply because they have rank in the Church or parish. We are all *beginners* with the elect, and they can help us to open our eyes to the possibility of pharisaism in our individual lives or in the life of the parish.

The Gospel makes it quite obvious that blindness (or any other affliction or disease) is not a punishment for sins of the individual or of his or her ancestors. Again, the weak in the eyes of the world gives God the opportunity to show forth divine power. The anointing the man receives in the Gospel is of mud, not of oil; and the name of the pool (*Siloam* meaning "One who has been sent") to which he is directed indicate that this saliva-and-earth anointing is just as much a commissioning, a sending, as is the anointing with chrism.

The dialogue with the Pharisees has been improperly interpreted as anti-Semitic. Rather it is directed against the self-righteous, and the division among the Pharisees shows that not all were persuaded that Jesus is not from God. The dialogue with the parents of the blind man shows their fear, a fear that will be fully realized in the Gospel account of Jesus' death.

The allegiance of the healed man to Jesus is ruthlessly questioned, another foreshadowing for the elect of the price they will have to pay for faithful adherence to Christ. The faith of the man is not the end of the story. The final words (John 9:41) are directed to those who think they are faithful but really are self-righteous. Claiming that they can see, they remain in darkness. It would be better that they were blind.

The prayer for the elect brings out the themes of the readings and again applies them to the elect and the parish, who are intimately bound together in this Lenten conversion process. The prayer of exorcism asks that the Lord bring these elect from any falsehood into the light of Christ. It is not to be assumed that the falsehoods are merely false religions, as some may assume who think this Rite is designed only for pagan countries or for those coming into light from pagan, non-Christian religions. Each of us believers has a litany of falsehoods that surround and blind us from which the Lord can exorcise us.

Life Eternal. Celebrated on the Fifth Sunday of Lent, the third scrutiny is immediate preparation for the feast of the Resurrection. The story of Jesus' raising Lazarus from the dead (John 11:1-44) has long been seen as a sign of the return to life of the Christ. The sign for this scrutiny is our actual coming to eternal life in Christ. It is tears turned into joy, the freeing of the dead Lazarus from the clothing of death. We do not stretch the imagination too much if we return to the former custom of covering the corpus of the crucifix with the shroud-like cloth as a visual point of reference.

Again emphasizing the theme of the Gospel, the first two readings are directed to the elect and the parish. Ezekiel's dry bones reading (37:1-14) can be fully given in the familiar song ("Ezechiel Cried Them Dry Bones") used as a response to the first reading which gives us only the conclusion to the popular reading. The selection from Romans 8:1-12 distinguishes between flesh that kills and Spirit that gives life. We will be brought to life through the same Spirit that raised Jesus from the dead.

The Gospel shows the friendship of Martha, Mary, and Lazarus with Jesus—a friendship to which we are all called. The fear of the disciples for Jesus' going back to Judea prepares us for the reading of the Passion on the next Sunday. But the overreaching theme is Jesus as the resurrection and the life. Lazarus will die again, and Jesus knows this. Jesus has saved all those who are incorporated in Him from death and oblivion.

The prayer for the *elect* petitions that they are united to Christ in His dying and rising and through the sacraments conquer the bitterness of death. One of the suggested petitions of the congregation recalls all those catechumens who have died for faith in the Lord. The seldom spoken of baptism of blood and desire is evoked.

The prayer of exorcism seeks freedom from the power of the evil spirit, who brings death, and a filling of the elect with the Holy Spirit, who brings life and gifts of faith, hope, and love.

The Rite of Christian Initiation directs that wherever the elect can be gathered on Holy Saturday, they should prepare themselves by recollection and prayer.

Until the nighttime liturgy of the Easter Vigil, Holy Saturday is the only day of the year when nothing but the Liturgy of the Hours is to be observed. The ritual suggests that the elect may listen to readings and a homily based on one or more of the following: the recitation of the Creed, the rite of *ephpheta* or opening of ears and mouth, the choosing of a Christian name, and the anointing with the oil of the catechumens (*RCIA*, 54).

On Holy Saturday in late morning, we gather the elect and, since it is their time to be together, offer them the option of inviting the parish. Normally they do so. A number of parishioners gather with the elect and their sponsors for a very informal service. Those decorating the church stop in the middle of what they are doing to join in the service. Some of the Easter lilies are spread across the floor of the sanctuary. A stepladder is left up. Clean altar linens and other things needed for the Vigil are halfway to their final destination. The atmosphere is of a relaxed dress rehearsal, and that is what we do as people arrive.

Daytime before Easter usually has even the elect running a little late. Places of seating and of the various Vigil activities are pointed out. Unconsecrated bread and wine for the Eucharist may be passed to the elect to sample texture and taste so that the signs lead not to themselves but to the deeper reality. We may even test the water temperature so that the newly baptized do not experience any chills. I still think Baptism water should be chilly for life-and-death symbolism. A vision of a cold waterfall on a warm Caribbean day stays planted in my mind. But I am regularly overruled by those who have to be baptized.

Then we settle down from who stands where and when and how we organize the Offertory procession.

Entering into a more reflective mood, we have the lectors for the evening read the readings we have chosen. Catechist or priest may give a very brief introduction or homily. We follow with a period of shared prayer which has become one of the staples of our whole process. The prayers are usually charged with anticipation as well as with a little nervousness.

Prior to this celebration, the priest has held the third face-to-face interview with the candidates, and it is amazing to hear the personal concerns, failings, and hopes of many of the elect being made public in this prayer session.

In the midst of all theological and catechetical controversy, everyone is agreed that the sacraments of initiation remove all previous sin from the unbaptized. Older Catholics are jokingly envious of the freshness with which the newly baptized adult begins the Christian life. It is therefore surprising to hear some unbaptized elect requesting the opportunity to confess their sins to a priest before the sacraments of initiation are received. Many make such a request, and many take advantage of the opportunity to make such confession if the chance if offered.

For those who have already been baptized and who are to be received, confirmed, and celebrate Eucharist completely, the former manner of reception during the Easter Vigil was to stop everything and have the newly received go off to a secluded spot with a priest for confession and sacramental absolution. They would finish, and the ceremony which had been frozen at that point would come back to life.

Greater theological minds than mine will have to settle whether or not the Eucharist is reconciliation enough for the already baptized who have moved through the rites of conversion of the catechumenate and the period of election. I believe that it more than suffices as a sacrament of healing and restoration and that it is the celebration of reconciliation as much as confession and sacramental forgiveness. Certainly for these who have given a year to the personal conversion process, the sacraments of initiation ought to suffice to forgive sins.

However, since all of our elect seem to want to spend some "holy time" in a review of life, we have not had to face the implications of this sacramental debate. We close our Holy Saturday prayer meeting by having a few priests available, literally to hear confessions. We take the "safe" approach with those already baptized and pray the words of forgiveness over them, with no penance but to continue as they have begun and to concentrate on the power shared with them through Christian initiation.

If there are persons who wish to review their life, a priest meets with them, and they talk. The meeting is concluded with a prayer for forgiveness in the saving waters of Baptism, a greeting of peace, and a prayer for dedication to the new way of life upon which the unbaptized are about to embark. Obviously this is not sacramental confession, and absolution is not given.

Here is a note to fellow confessors for what it is worth: be prepared during this "personal review" to spend twice the time you may normally expect, because the elect have a way of going deeper into their lives than does the baptized penitent in confession. Sometimes questions of an important nature which have never surfaced before come up at this time. The review of life may well bring up some unsettling and upsetting events in past life which require the best of your healing efforts.

Use of the Rite of Christian Initiation at Saints Paul

and Augustine parish has taught a lesson that liturgists and the pastorally inclined are trying to teach without using the Rite. It is that the nature of Lent is that of a season that begins with a call to repentance and conversion. Readings and prayers of the Sundays, of the daily Eucharists, and of the Hours; the fasting and the works of justice and mercy—all are a confrontation with the conscience of the individual and the community of faith.

The confrontation with the standards of Christ and the Gospel is a constructive, converting process that should not be rushed by a parish celebration of Reconciliation early in Lent; or else the purpose of Lent is defeated. The time for the celebration of Reconciliation is no earlier than Holy Week and probably best celebrated on the feast of the Lord's Supper. But pastoral judgment that takes into account all the conditions of the parish may well decide on another day in Holy Week.

What the elect have taught us is that their use of the whole of Lent to accomplish a final conversion to the Lord and the process for us who are seeking to celebrate our reinitiation are processes to be achieved in tandem. They are to be achieved in a manner that binds the elect and the total parish in the same work and heightens the urgency for the "old-timers" to get their lives and priorities in order so as to serve as a living example to the elect.

[5] *Gospel According to John*, Nos. 29 and 29a. The "Anchor Bible" Series. Garden City, Doubleday, 1966, 1970. Also *The Community of the Beloved Disciple*, Paulist Press, N.Y., 1979.

Easter Vigil

WE will not go through the Easter Vigil service step by step. It is all too familiar as the high point of our liturgical life. The prominent presence of those about to be initiated increases the expectant mood of the whole parish. This is a celebration of the corporate, communitarian sense of salvation. The parish meets in the darkness of night (please, not in twilight!) to celebrate the victory of the Lord over sin and death. The experience is of *our* being saved, not of *my* being saved. We are being made into a new people, swelled by the incorporation of the elect; and to the degree that we are intimately united to this family of faith and to the whole Church, we realize that we stand together with the Lord in the newness of life. The Lord is making us new in His image.

All the elements bring the sense of newness, of rededication, and of commitment to working for the kingdom. New fire, new candle, incense, new water, immersion and sprinkling, robes of the newly baptized, oil, prayers, readings—all correspond to a sense of the newness of spring. Is it too much to hope that vestments, sanctuary decorations, banners, and music combine to bring about a sense of being born again?

Here in this evening we have the ancient practice of Christian initiation restored. With the whole assembly we move through fire, candle, litany of the saints, water, chrism, and Eucharist in the order in which they were originally celebrated. This rite is not going back for the sake of tradition. This night is an experience of how these sacraments fit together so well to achieve a sense of salvation. We can feel and sense what the Church means when saying that in the Rite of Christian Initiation of Adults we have the norm for Christian initiation.

For so many of us baptized at infancy, who have labored to make the revised rite of infant Baptism as meaningful as possible, it is no secret that the Easter Vigil celebration of Christian initiation overshadows infant Baptism celebrations in intensity and significance. To be part of the Easter Vigil celebration is to realize and appreicate what you missed in your mother's arms or what you cannot hope to simulate within the content of a Sunday Eucharist.

After the Vigil our parish hosts a true break-fast which serves to break the fast of the preceding two days and to hold a reception for the new members. Food (great quantities of food), champagne, music, and even dancing are part of the festivities designed to continue the spirit of the Easter Vigil.

In our parish, attendance at Mass on Easter Sunday is double normal Sunday attendance. Many are "occasional" Catholics who rise to the occasion of Easter. Many are unaffiliated non-Catholics who feel a need to be in a church on Easter Sunday. All are welcome. The choirs return from the Vigil festivities to one of the Easter Sunday Eucharists. We encourage parishioners to do likewise. But we push the neophytes, those newly initiated, to return to one or other of our later Easter Sunday Eucharists. They are introduced and prayed for, and their visibility provides the occasion to invite interested "inquirers" to begin the process of Christian initiation by attending the sessions of post-baptismal catechesis under absolutely no obligation.

The elect, the chosen of the Lord, are always at work, giving as a gift what they have received as a gift.

Fourth Stage:
Postbaptismal Catechesis or Mystagogia

Deeper into the Mystery

THE word *mystagogia,* used to describe this period, is awesome and strange even for the student of New Testament Greek. It can scare off even the persistent. "What is all this about *mystagogia?*"

You are reading the work of one who once thought this word and the goals of this final period of initiation quite obscure. *Mystagogia* is a forceful word for "mystery," but the mystery is God's initiative, not the whys and hows of structuring a period of coming to know something in a deeper, more experiential way.

We have renamed this period "Deeper into the Mystery." This period is not one of "me and my notebook," as indeed the whole process of Christian initiation cannot be compared to the formal system of college or graduate work. This period is for experiencing the family history as our own, a time for celebrating the power that the Lord has shared in allowing us to be called His daughters and sons. This is a seven-week period of coming home for the first time. The *mystagogia* is the full Easter-to-Pentecost season, a celebration of a particular community of faith that has grown close to new members who have come to share the full experience of the family's reason for existence.

"The time of postbaptismal catechesis is of great importance so that the neophytes, helped by their sponsors, may enter into a closer relationship with the faithful and bring them renewed vision and a new impetus" (*RCIA,* 39). Every member of the family of faith gets into the Easter spirit of making the new members feel at home. Only when the neophytes feel "at home" can they comfortably bring the family renewed vision of what being "in Christ" means to them. The sense of familiarity, of being welcome, can lead the parish family to feel a new impetus for the works of the kingdom. The Rite makes it clear that every parish should regularly be treated to such an experiencing of new life.

The question, as always, is how best to provide the atmosphere for such sharing. The Rite suggests that the main place for the postbaptism catechesis is the Sunday Eucharistic liturgy. Again it recommends the readings from the Year A Cycle (*RCIA*, 40). But to reduce these Eucharists to the simple celebration of Mass is not intended. The readings and the homily are directed to creating a mood in which the neophytes and their sponsors can freely speak to the family assembly of the personal impact of initiation. This goal takes time and sensitivity on the part of liturgical planners. Surely the parish has to feel the importance of hearing from the neophytes, and this communication may mean recasting expectations that the Sunday liturgy of the neophytes will conclude in fifty minutes.

Not every neophyte or sponsor need to speak each Sunday of Easter. At Saints Paul and Augustine parish we continue the once-a-week evening sessions during this period and create a festive atmosphere by adding more refreshments to the normal coffee and tea. Hearing the readings for the approaching Sunday leads easily into discussion of the personal impact of the sacramental encounters with Christ. From these weekly sessions, catechist and pastor/priest select stories and insights worth repeating at the Sunday celebrations. The sponsors' experiences gained from close association with the neophytes are valuable and intimately related to the purpose of the season. They should be heard on Sunday as well.

By Pentecost the Eucharistic assembly should have heard from every neophyte and sponsor at least once. What is missed in these personal presentations can be included in the homilies by an alert priest or deacon. The General Intercessions should also reflect the personal insights and faith-sharing of the neophytes. They should also include the prayer that the enthusiasm of the neophytes becomes contagious. The neophytes are the ministers of the Easter season to the whole parish.

As we become more sophisticated and experienced in the use of this process of Christian initiation, we should be able to provide more and more for the active involvement of the whole parish family in these sessions. Without making the Sunday Eucharist a string of personal testimonies from each and every member of the Eucharistic assembly, we can provide more and more opportunities for those so inclined to express their feelings. True, too many dialogue homilies could become "head trips" of believers making intellectual points and counterpoints and could "turn off" those who are rightly searching for the experience of Christianity. Yet we do need to find more and more ways for neophytes and longtime members of the family to express why they believe and where they find their personal supports for faith.

Bringing the neophytes and their sponsors into adult religious education programs during this time can only enrich those programs and prompt the participant to some sort of personal response beyond "That's nice." The neophytes can pump new life into programs of parental preparation for their children's celebration of Confirmation, First Communion, and

Reconciliation. They can set parents to a stimulating participation and exchange with the neophytes because of their interest in the neophytes and their concern to bring their children to active faith.

Some of the most rewarding interactions during this fifty-day celebration are between the neophytes and those whose initiation may have been delayed to Pentecost because of their own decision or because they entered the program at a later date. The encouragement to push on is tangible. Not to be missed are the possibilities inherent in the neophytes sitting with interested inquirers and assisting and strenghtening their desire at least to try the precatechumenate phase which will begin immediately after Pentecost. This fifty-day celebration is much more than a party or an extended reception. It is the beginning of recognition that the neophytes and their sponsors exercise a crucial and important ministry in the life of the parish.

Entering Ministries

SPEAKING of ministries, we consider the Easter season the appropriate time to formalize the entry of the neophytes into the ministries they have chosen and those for which the parish has the greatest need. Both aspects are important. The neophyte should be able to choose a ministry within the local parish to which he or she is attracted. But the parish also has a duty to insure that needed ministries are being performed. Perhaps the best way to achieve these ends is to have the representative body of the parish, the parish council, assess during the Lenten season the performance and the functioning of its various ministries. Then, in the spirit of the Easter celebration, the parish council should dialogue with the neophytes on their experiences and hear their preferences regarding participation in one or another parish ministry. If much needed work is not being performed, perhaps for sick and shut-ins, the council should realize its responsibility and persuade some of the neophytes to enter upon this work, while at the same time performing other ministries to which they may naturally be drawn.

Sometimes we give the impression that selecting and performing a liturgical ministry in, say, lectoring or music, is choice enough. We tend to forget that every liturgical ministry has to have a corresponding and correlative ministry during the week, or else the liturgical experience occurs in a vacuum. Seeing weekly and Sunday ministries together is among the more profound bases of liturgical reform.

The parish should have a complete list of ministries currently performed and ministries that need to be organized. This listing should be the product of the parish council's Lenten assessment of the state of the parish family in the light of the call to conversion. From this listing the neophyte should choose a ministry or ministries, and from it the parish council should insure that the work of the parish goes forward. We have not yet reached this point of parochial organization and ministerial selection, but the future is bright, and the possibility is at hand.

Beyond the actual workings of this final phase of the initiatory process, there are deeper implications for the life of the Church, as indeed there are from the other periods. Just as Lent is given its reason for being the time for total conversion of parish and personal life by the presence of the elect, so the Easter season is given a much fuller life by the mutual interaction of neophyte and parish. The presence of a group being incorporated into the life and ministry of a parish family enables us to see the interrelatedness of the seasons of Lent and Easter.

Easter and Lent! A fifty-day celebration of what it means to be risen in Christ prepared for by a forty-day observance of fasting and prayerful consideration of the priorities and the price of being a true Christian! We are traditionally more preoccupied with the Lenten season than with the Easter season. In so many of our parishes Easter is the exclamation point for Lent, and the fervor grinds to a halt. No more crowds at daily Mass, no resolutions, no special parish programs are features of Easter. It is as if we know better the language and practice of self-denial, repentance, and even guilt than the upbeat activities of living a new life in Christ.

In fact, a national committee recently working on a spirituality statement for American priests found that the clergy generally could think of more synonyms and expressions to speak about the dying of Jesus than they could about the rising of Christ. We seem to have left the field of new life, of being risen in Christ to the born-again variety of Christians. These facts may account for the popularity of the charismatic movement in many Catholic communities.

The revised Rite of Christian Initiation compels Catholics to come to grips with the vital implications of Christ's having put death and sin behind us. The presence of the newly initiated exercising the beginnings of their ministry in the parish will greatly assist parishes in bringing their Easter celebration up to par with Lenten practice. And there is no special programmatic for either season beyond hearing the Word as proclaimed in Eucharistic gatherings and acting in accord with what is heard and experienced.

These ninety days, one fourth of the calendar year, beginning with Ash Wednesday or the First Sunday of Lent and concluding with Pentecost, is the Church's short course to itself on the nature and meaning of Christian life. In a very direct way the precatechumenate and the catechumenate phases are valuable only as the preparation for these ninety days of the corporate dying and rising experience with the Lord.

Mystagogia and Evangelization

THE *mystagogia* teaches us, too, that catechesis is not what we may have been led to believe. The enterprise is not information for the sake of "getting it right." No series of texts for the young replete with parent handbooks, no catechist expected to cover a book in a semester or year, no matter how well trained, can show what traditional catechesis really is. Ultimately catechesis has nothing to do with texts or tests except for the Bible and meeting the tests of life. There is no question that the revitalization of the catechetical field for the young and parent preparation courses for first sacraments has added a vitality to the life of our parishes. Catholics know more about their religion, Scripture, and liturgy than they did a generation ago. But the coming to faith of an adult believer cannot be commercialized or captured in any single set of books.

The revised Rite of Christian Initiation, where it is being implemented, has begun to catechize the Church, to catechize us about the process and life of catechesis itself. Postbaptismal catechesis is a living example that Christians who share their experiences of life—and how their faith forms, structures, and deepens those life experiences—are catechizing one another. Catechesis is present only when more and more Catholics in this or that parish are bringing one another to faith.

No one person can be catechist; no one priest can lead anyone to the total truth. Catechesis is a ministry of the *whole* parish. Father Smith may be able to instruct Jackson, but the parish forms Jackson into the kind of believer Jackson will be. If the parish is strong in its identity with Christ and His work, Jackson the neophyte should be also. If the parish family has not come to grips with its basic reason for being, our Jackson will be alone in spite of all of Father Smith's instructions. The parish is the former of Catholic Christians. As the revised Rite is tried and increasingly put into practice, more and more members of the parish will realize their formative role not only in the lives of new Christians but also in the lives of one another.

Lastly, the *mystagogia* teaches the evangelical importance of Easter. The celebration of the Resurrection of the Lord is not an "in-house" service. What the Christ has done for each and every one of us has a consequence. Once celebrated, Easter is a gift that has to be given. Neophytes multiply themselves. Sponsors grow confident in their ministry. The source of true evangelization is uncovered and cannot be kept secret. If we "sit" on what has been received and celebrated, it goes stale. Salvation has to be shared, or it becomes a hoarded treasure to be guarded and the source of self-righteousness, a sin that Jesus never ceased to condemn.

The neophytes add more than an impetus to the evangelical nature of the Easter event. They crystallize in new and fresh ways the experience of salvation. Part of our problem as Catholics has been an ethereal definition of salvation and redemption. We have heard the words so often that we have come to equate them with heaven. How surprised we are when the person in the next pew says that salvation means a complete change in the way he or she approaches life. When the garden club is replaced by Scripture study, when the donation to charity becomes an afterthought to the service to be performed for the one in need in front of you, then the definition of salvation begins to take a more earthly form. When persons who used to fear strangers and never would let anyone get too close are now ready to endure the possibility of being hurt in opening themselves to one another, then salvation comes down to earth. When the owner of closets full of clothes and the latest model car can say people are more important than things and he is ready to volunteer two nights a week in youth work, then salvation becomes flesh and blood.

We do what we do because of Easter. And because of Easter we encourage one another to keep doing for the sake of a new creation.

Epilogue: A Year After

THE Rite of Christian Initiation of Adults is the process whereby the Church brings persons to Christ and Christ to those who have begun to believe. The most important, the most significant element in the process is the local faith community, i.e. the parish. The parish is the sacrament of the entire Church for the inquirer, for the catechumen. The whole parish is vital to the process. The parish is truly an agent of the total incorporating, conversion experience.

The Rite should not be attempted by a parish only vaguely aware of itself. The variety of parish lay ministries should be functioning at least in a "first stage" fashion before a parish decides to introduce the Rite. Parish council members will explain what the council is attempting to achieve; parish organization heads will do likewise and thereby justify the purpose of their organization (maybe). Lectors, social services ministers, teachers, priests, religious, Eucharistic ministers—all become active in the process as does the worshiping congregation.

If there is one constant in the process, one jewel in the Rite, it is that each parish, each community of faith, is going to adapt the process according to its own best pastoral judgment. Once the Rite is established in parishes and dioceses have called parishes together to share their experiences, comparisons between parishes and their catechumenates cannot become competitive. Thoughtful pastoral teams, catechists, and sponsors will take very different approaches based on their needs, their situation, and their experience with the Rite.

Adaptations will vary widely along economic, intellectual, cultural and, even, ethnic lines. Our own experience at Saints Paul and Augustine is best received by others when we describe what we attempt to do, not as a prescription for you, but as meeting a need or filling a gap for our parish. Your situation will be different, perhaps very different, from ours. The faith is still one, holy, catholic, and apostolic.

Since this was written, we have decided to follow the Rite in publicly excusing catechumens after the General Intercessions of our principal Sunday Eucharist. Our thoughts or fears of rejection were unfounded. The presence of catechumens for the Liturgy of the Word is the best communal, prayerful beginning for a weekly "session" because it starts with the parish at prayer and develops a sense of belonging from the membership stage of the process.

The departure of the catechumens also serves as a sign to the parish that a number of persons are seriously interested in as complete a conversion experience as possible. Their leaving is a weekly reminder that this order of parish members is committed to at least another hour of sharing, reflecting, and praying, another hour beyond the emptying of the parking lot at the conclusion of the principal Mass.

We changed. We adapted the Rite to meet an exclusivist or rejecting tendency by not excusing catechumens. Now we are following the Rite and gaining much more. We gained a sense of the Rite being liturgical, part of the Church's prayer life even outside the sanctuary or the church building. We gained an appreciation of the parallels between the variety of ministries in the total parish, in its liturgical experience and in its catechumenate. But I can only hasten to add that, if a parish thought excusing catechumens after the General Intercessions went "against the grain," then suit yourself. You may reach a collective decision to do otherwise "down the road." Stay open. Evaluate. Listen. Share with others.

It should be clear that the Rite is not for terminally ill parishes to "operate." It is for parishes who have attempted the reforms of Vatican II. Introduction of the Rite should not be geared chiefly to recycling Catholics or recycling parishes. Such recycling may be a welcome by-product, but the work of the Rite is too important, too much a part of the ongoing life of a parish, to be allowed to become another piece in an adult religious education program. The catechumenate, the Rite, has enough to do to provide the process for complete incorporation into the parish and all that implies. Do not weigh it down or belittle it by making it your adult religious education program or your marriage preparation program or your panacea for parish revitalization.

You can learn from *RCIA* about some other things you do. You can learn the difference between catechesis proper and religious education. You can learn as we have that if Baptism, Confirmation, and Eucharist are the climax celebrations of initiation, then piecemeal preparation of parents for their children's celebration of these mysteries probably makes little sense. The Church is clear on how to view Christian initiation. Look at how adults are initiated. At the very least, then, parents of youngsters to be baptized, confirmed, "eucharisted," and, perhaps, reconciled, should see the process as a whole, and not as disjointed and punctuated by a series of repeated preparations of each parent for each child's celebration of each sacrament.

We have organized an adjunct program for parents of youngsters whose time has come for whatever of the four sacraments: Baptism, Confirmation, Eucharist, Reconciliation. The design is a modified design of the Rite of Christian Initiation that lays out the sacramental experiences in their proper adult chronological order.

This process exposes the inconsistencies of our current sacramental practice and the need for continuing reform of how the Church brings its young to full stature in Christ. Some inconsistencies point to the delightful humanness of our Church and are surely tolerable until such a time as the Church reaches consensus on its sacramental practice for the twenty-first century. In my mind, other inconsistencies require immediate remedies or the whole tradition of the Church may be lost. The floating age of Confirmation from diocese to diocese in these United States threatens the very integrity of the sacrament itself. It is gratifying to know that our bishops are studying the problem.

Each of these considerations could provide ample material for another book. The implications of implementing the Rite are enormous for this writer. Try the Rite in your parish. Be courageous. The Rite will not fail you. Some study, a careful reading of the Rite, a willingness to share your experiences and to refashion and adapt—those are the simple requirements. Each cycle is different; each group has its own chemistry. The Rite has not failed. Thank you for your time.